Bluegills!

Bluegills!

By Dave Genz, with Mark Strand

Part of the Winter Fishing Systems
Cutting Edge Ice Fishing Series

Beaver's Pond Press, Inc.

Published by Beaver's Pond Press
Edina, Minnesota

ISBN: 1-890676-48-9

Library of Congress Catalog Card Number: 99-067685

First Edition

First Printing: October 1999

Printed in the United States of America

05 04 03 02 01 00   6 5 4 3 2 1

Written & edited by Dave Genz and Mark Strand
Cover Photo by Mark Strand
Layout & Design by Mark Strand
Illustrations by Sheila Dahlberg

Published by Beaver's Pond Press, Inc.
5125 Danen's Drive
Edina, Minnesota 55439-1465

To order additional copies of Bluegills!
Call toll-free 1-877-328-0488. VISA and MasterCard accepted. Or, send check or money order for $11.95 plus $3 shipping, to:
Winter Fishing Systems, 5930 - 16th Ave. SE, St. Cloud, MN 56304.
Canadian orders: Please make sure payment is in U.S. funds, and shipping becomes $6.

To all you ice anglers who love

to chase bluegills

on frozen waters

Foreword

What would you give to sit down, one-on-one, and talk fishing with Dave Genz, the guy who changed ice fishing forever?

I consider myself the luckiest ice fisherman on the face of the earth. You see, I get to do that. We fish together. We ride together on long trips to go fishing. We meet for lunch. He's as gracious and unpretentious and so completely lacking an ego that it's sometimes hard to imagine that this guy is a celebrity.

Oh, in some circles he won't be recognized. But anywhere ice anglers gather, they know the Fish Trap and the Ice Box and the new way of ice fishing, and they know Dave Genz.

To sit and talk with him is to understand why he is the foremost authority on ice fishing. Even in the heat of summer, sweat dripping down his forehead, he's talking about ice fishing. He has those special instincts of all great fishermen, the technical knack of an inventor, and the vision of an entrepreneur, all wrapped into this humble friendliness that belies it all.

This book is Dave Genz on bluegills through the ice. That's like a book by Mark McGuire on how to hit the ball over the fence, or Frank Sinatra on singing. We can't all hope to catch fish just like Dave does, because he has a gift for it. But his System will make you one mean fish-catchin' machine, even if you've struggled in the past.

He wants to share what he knows, so you can catch more big bluegills. He's so open about offering his insights that the pressure is on me to draw out the most important information and get it down clearly.

My goal was simple with this book: make it seem like a one-on-one conversation with Dave Genz on ice fishing for bluegills. He's going to tell you how to understand these fish, how to get the right equipment, how to dress for it, how to find the right spots, and how to catch fish once you're sitting over the top of them.

Dave has a lot to say. I hope little light bulbs come on in your head the whole time you're reading it. And I also hope that, once you begin catching bigger bluegills, that you let most of the big ones go.

— Mark Strand

Preface

Nobody learns in a vacuum. Nobody becomes better as a fisherman by only fishing alone. There are so many people who have fished with me, and spent hours talking fishing with me, since the early days, when the Fish Trap was invented, and we started using depthfinders through the ice.

You'll hear me say 'we' a lot in this book, as I refer to the system 'we' use, and the things 'we' have learned about bluegills. I have a huge network of friends and fellow anglers, that I owe a huge thank-you to. The list is far too long, and offers too many chances to forget somebody important, so I'm not going to even attempt it. I do want to mention my wife Patsy, who has been my partner in life and helps me do everything I do; my daughters, Melissa and Kathy, who worked assembling Fish Traps in our garage in the early days with a cheerful attitude; Rick & Judy Johnson; and my uncle, Eugene Lease, who in the 1950s first built a Fish Trap-style fish house, and inspired me with all his great ideas.

Without all of you, and all the time we spend together on the ice, my career in ice fishing would never have become a dream realized.

— Dave Genz

Acknowledgments

The authors wish to thank Patsy Genz and Jill Strand for the unselfish support needed during the long hours required to bring a book to life. They also both want to express their appreciation for the time and attention given to them early in life by their fathers, who got them started in fishing.

Thanks also to Dennis Clark, President of Clam Corp and creator of Ice Team, a progressive organization helping to drive the growth in the great sport of ice fishing; to all the staff of Clam Corp., Strikemaster, Vexilar, Berkley, and Lindy-Little Joe; to Mac Strand, Ph.D., professor of entomology and aquatic ecology at Northern Michigan University, for help understanding the dynamics of a frozen-over lake, and the behavior of food items bluegills prey on in winter. His scientific training, along with a lifetime of ice fishing for bluegills, makes him qualified to explain why things happen the way they do, which can help us all become better anglers, and better stewards of the environment.

Contents

CHAPTER ONE

BLUEGILLS!

We chase big bluegills. It's one of the things we do. Really, it's part of what we are. Miles mean nothing when you set the hook on a bluegill and it takes some time to decide who's boss.

Our ice fishing adventures take us to lakes that look interesting on the map, or wherever the best rumors are. Things don't always work out, and we drill lots of holes in plenty of lakes that end up having nothing but average fish. But it's the spirit of adventure that keeps us going, looking for that next honest pounder—a fish that weighs 16 full ounces on an accurate scale. We've found a few waters holding bluegills that push two pounds and beyond, and to those places we sometimes caravan, strings of Minnesota license plates pushing through the wind and the blowing snow.

We stay in hotels that are not exactly the Ritz, and we sit around in t-shirts and rig up tackle and tell stories, and that's half the fun, too. Ice fishing has become a whole new sport in the recent past. It has become exciting to gear up with state-of-the-art stuff, and really get into playing the game.

Late into the night, we share ideas on where bluegills might be, and what it takes to trigger them into biting, and we keep it up at breakfast the next morning. We've even taken to using radios to talk back and forth between vehicles as we drive to the lake. We talk about other stuff sometimes, but most of the time we talk about fishing.

Fishing is the ultimate lifetime sport, and bluegills are the ultimate lifetime fish. When you start out, it's easy to find eager biters that bring you consistent success. Then, as you progress, the pursuit of slabs, bulls, becomes an obsession.

It was on a frozen gravel road in South Dakota that the idea for this book was born, while we were on our way to the lake, talking about updating my seminar program, and wondering what else we could do to help people catch more fish, and become better ice fishermen. It might take a book, we thought. Maybe it was time for a whole book on nothing but bluegills.

Yeah, it's time.

Still, you know what they say about fishing books. You can only learn so much from reading. You have to get out there and fish to really learn. I won't argue with that. But hopefully this book will help you cut through a lot of trial and error.

I remember that morning, when we were hatching the idea for this book. I can still see the lake in the distance, a big white flat spot in the middle of endless cattails and snow-swept prairie. There have been so many lakes, some like that one and others very different. The common thread is that our system works on bluegills no matter where you go.

I've heard it from so many people that it comes to me in my sleep: *our bluegills are different. Those jigs won't work here. You have to do such-and-such or you won't catch any fish.* Now that I've put in my time traveling west to east and north to south across the ice belt, fishing in every type of water imaginable, I can say it with more confidence than ever: our system works no matter where you go. We've refined it, and I can say that about the only differences come from whether the fish are in clear water or dirty, shallow or deep.

The essential system remains the same wherever we go, shining all the more because it's versatile. No matter what type of water you fish 'gills in—natural lakes big and small, backwaters of rivers and reservoirs, ponds or pits—you'll find it discussed, and our system will catch fish there.

Bluegills of at least decent size are available pretty much anywhere water freezes over. But when you get the big bluegill bug, you have to go where big bluegills live. Accessibility to the spot regulates the size of the fish in many instances; if it's easy for lots of people to get there, the size gets fished down, especially on smaller waters. If the lake is heavily fished, people can't seem to help themselves—they keep the big ones, and pretty soon the biggest ones are smaller than they used to be. But with waters that are remote, private, hard to get to, controlled well—or sometimes a lake in an area going through a high-water cycle—bluegills can get big.

We always say that finding the right lake is a big part of the hunt. But on any day, on any water, to catch any bluegills, you have to find them first. Otherwise, the most sophisticated presentation on earth isn't going to work.

In more ways than one, it's location, location, location.

That's a critical concept to understand. Still, it may not be the most important thing of all. The most important thing of all may be this:

Your bluegills are not any different from my bluegills.

CHAPTER TWO

THE SYSTEM...AS IT PERTAINS TO BLUEGILLS

The somewhat-older gentleman cut a classic figure, standing there like he represented a thousand years of ice fishing tradition, apparently unwilling to budge off his spot. If it were late in the season, ice would be slowly melting around the outline of his boots.

As it was, his bobber was bobbing in a hole from which only two little sunnies had been produced all afternoon. Still, he stood there, so accepting of his fate and his place—after all, he was an ice fisherman—that he was smiling, not one thought of drilling another hole someplace else.

At his request, we showed him our fish, six nice bluegills from among 40 or so we'd caught in a few hours. He didn't appear to buy it when we told him we'd actually let the biggest fish go.

We encouraged him, showed him how our Fish Traps and FL-8s worked, showed him that no fish were in his hole. We told him the catchable 'gills were about a foot off the bottom, and they wanted it jigged aggressively. Showed him our graphite rods, and our jigs, and how to hook a maggie so it wiggled.

"Man," he said, "you guys want heaven on earth."

Some people might see it as heaven on earth, but it's here, right now, more refined than ever, waiting for you to try. I call it my Winter Fishing System. I still get people coming up to me at seminars and asking what the System is. It's not difficult to explain, but it does take a while.

Here, I'm going to specifically describe the system as it pertains to bluegills, right down to the rods, reels, line and baits that will make you efficient at searching for—and catching—fish every time out. Essentially, the System remains the same as you fish through the ice for other species, except for rods, line, lures, and bait.

At its very core, the Winter Fishing System mimics, as closely as possible, the best assets of fishing out of a boat during the open-water season. We search the lake for structural elements, find fish, present a bait to them, move quickly from spot to spot, and stay comfortable while we're at it. What we discover is that this System of ice fishing actually has several important advantages over fishing out of a boat, which we'll explain as we go.

The System changes ice fishing from the way most people used to do it: namely, drill one hole and sit out on a bucket, no matter what the weather, and wait for fish to come to them.

When you break down the System, you find elements to it, and it makes sense what we're trying to accomplish. You see why we've created certain pieces of equipment, and why refinements to existing equipment were critical to the way we fish today.

Mobility

Our success as ice anglers hinges on being able to move, unless you happen to fish in some lake that I don't know about, where you can drill one hole and catch the biggest fish in the lake every time out.

Like every aspect of the System, we begin with the problem and come up with the solution. In this case, the problem has always been that ice anglers don't move enough. They either hauled a permanent shelter onto a spot and fished there all winter, or drilled one hole and sat there all day on a bucket.

If we knew where all the big fish were, and they were all in one place, we'd only have to drill one hole. In reality, fish are scattered and they move as conditions change. So we have to move, too, and drill more than one hole. When you think about it, the ability to quickly cut a hole through the ice didn't exist until recently—so the perceived hassle of making new holes has always been another factor that kept people from moving. Augers used to be stone-age instruments compared to the modern Lazers we use now. So even if a guy had all his gear in a five-gallon bucket and could move, he wasn't inclined to move, because it was hard work to drill another hole.

If it's easy to move, you will; if it isn't, you won't. Never is this more true than in the winter, when you get all snugly and warm inside a permanent fish house. The thought of packing everything up and moving it to another spot is not nearly as appealing as dealing another hand of gin rummy.

If it's easy to move, you will...

What it came down to was we needed a fish house that functioned like a boat. It had to hold everything we needed for a day of fishing, keep it dry and protected, and skim over the ice like a boat skims across the water. It had to pull easily behind a person walking,

---

so legs could provide the only source of mobility for those who don't have snowmobiles or ATVs.

That's how the Fish Trap was born. Out of the desire for mobility in ice fishing. Suddenly, we had a plastic sled with runners, carpeted dry storage for our gear, a rod rack to protect our high-quality ice rods, and canvas walls that flipped up around us at the flick of a wrist. Virtually instant setup and takedown. That's what you need.

If it's easy to move, you will; if it isn't, you won't.

After we created this dream shelter for mobile ice anglers, most people still found a way to make it into virtually a permanent house. The sled is able to hold a lot of stuff, so ice anglers packed stuff into it until the sled was full. Guess what happens if you do that? It becomes too heavy to pull easily. It becomes a hassle to move, so they sit in one spot all day, even though they're fishing out of a Fish Trap.

You can make anything into an anchor if you put enough stuff in it.

But used the way it's intended to be used, a Fish Trap makes it easy to move from spot to spot as you hunt for fish.

A Fish Trap—if it's packed light—makes it easy to move.

You might argue that putting your stuff into a five-gallon bucket makes for good mobility. In a way it does, although you have to carry your auger, because it won't fit in a bucket. And how many days is it comfortable to sit outside on a bucket? Even if you're dressed warmly enough, ice usually forms in your guides in short order, making it difficult to fish well. And even when you can stay warm enough, how fun is it to have the wind blowing your line around while you're trying to detect bites? Oh, and your rod tips are sticking out of the bucket, where they can more easily be broken. And when you go to sit down, you often have to empty everything out of the bucket and lay it down in the snow.

I'll take a Fish Trap over a five-gallon bucket any day. On those rare perfect days, I can flip the top up and I'm sitting outside, with my gear at my fingertips. I can (and often do) move quickly from hole to hole, kneeling to fish, my Fish Trap close by, ready to haul all my gear at my whim, without having to be packed up.

The Top 10 reasons for continuing to ice fish on a five-gallon bucket:

10. Finger sensation is not all it's cracked up to be.

9. It's fun to have things burning in your pocket.

8. Any wimp can detect bites when their line isn't blowing around.

7. It's fun to pack 10 gallons of stuff into a 5-gallon bucket.

6. Sometimes, the swirling winds give you a presentation that's impossible to duplicate inside a Fish Trap.

5. By studying the chunks of ice forming on your line, you can get in touch with your artistic side.

4. You learn a lot of new dance steps.

3. You've learned to enjoy feeling grumpy.

2. You'll never miss a chance to ask other people if it's cold enough for 'em.

1. It puts you on the fast track to that ruddy complexion.

The System...As It Pertains to Bluegills

Mobility has come in other forms, too. We want to cover long distances, so we either put the Fish Traps in the back of a truck and drive, slip the rope over the trailer hitch of the truck and drive, snowshoe or ski or let the dog pull the Trap, or create a state-of-the-art ice fishing machine from a specialized snowmobile.

The Right Snowmobile

If you get the right snowmobile for ice fishing, you get extreme mobility, faster than most boats, in fact. Unless the ice is rough, you can cover ground in a hurry. Any snowmobile will do, within reason, but here's what to look for in a mean ice-fishing machine:

* A wide-track, long-track, with high- and low-range transmission. That type of machine has the ability to pull at slow speeds (with the low range), and high speeds.

* I like a liquid-cooled engine, because it doesn't heat up easily.

* Find a local machine shop that will build you a rack that nests a Fish Trap sled. Set your Trap into the "nest," strap your auger on, and away you go.

* Rig a GPS onto a bracket on the dash. You're a machine.

* This type of snowmobile can also pull a trailer loaded down with Fish Traps and people, believe it or not. The secret is to have the machine shop create custom skiis that the wheels of the trailer nest into.

* We use ATVs (4-wheelers), too, but they aren't as efficient on snow. Basically, they can't go anywhere your truck can't go, except for the weight factor. Apples to apples, a snowmobile is a much better tool for ice fishing than an ATV.

We've even used bicycles in situations where motorized transportation wasn't allowed, such as in National Wildlife Refuges. Some of the refuge lakes are big, and good fishing can be had beyond the limits of easy walking distance.

One good bike for ice fishing is a mountain bike with thin, studded tires.

You want narrow—not fat—tires, because they give you better traction on any snow. When it comes to snow, realize that when get beyond a bit, you can't use a bike, because they just don't plow through the white stuff. For us older guys, I am working on an idea for a three-wheeled bicycle that could pull a Fish Trap.

Mike "Bummer" O'Neil, of Stillwater, MN, with a big bull 'gill that came from a National Wildlife Refuge lake. He used studded tires on a mountain bike to get around on the ice, which was relatively free of snow.

You see, this all comes from the desire to move in order to catch more fish. Previous generations of ice anglers didn't move much at all. Now, we move as much as we have to in order to find the fish we want, and then we zero in on a specific spot and have some fun catching.

We'll talk about depthfinders more when we discuss the presentation portion of the System, but it's important to say a few words about what they've meant to mobility. Being able to use depthfinders through the ice—or through a hole cut in the ice—has allowed us the luxury of meaningful mobility. It doesn't mean anything to move unless you're moving somewhere in particular, unless you're checking shallow weeds, then mid-depth weeds, then deeper basins, then points, then humps, and so on.

Movement for the sake of movement is not the mobility we're talking about here. It's critical to quickly determine how deep the water is in the new spot, whether there are any weeds or other elements of cover, whether there are any fish present, whether there are any microorganisms present, and how hard or soft the bottom is. Using a state-of-the-art depthfinder (my hands-down choice is the Vexilar FL-8), rigged for ice fishing, makes meaningful mobility possible.

So far, we haven't been able to create the right combination of gear to provide a high-speed depthfinder reading while we're moving across the ice (the way you can read a depthfinder in a boat while it's moving across the water), so it does take longer in the winter to find the tip of a point or a clump of weeds. But once you do find what you're looking for, it's easier to sit on top of the spot.

Remember I said there are certain important advantages in ice fishing over fishing from a boat? This is one of the biggest. Boat control, staying over a spot, is not an issue. You find the edge of a clump of weeds and it has bluegills in it, you can sit right there and worry only about your presentation.

As you check depths and look down a weedline, for example, you can write the depths in the snow or leave something sitting on the ice marking your key spots. Advantage ice angler!

Warmth/Comfort

Ice anglers have another huge advantage over people fishing out of a boat any time the weather is less than ideal. I'll stack up the comfort factor of ice fishing, on the average day, against the comfort factor of being out in a boat if it's raining, really windy, and even slightly cold. I think it takes a much hardier soul to fish in the early spring or late fall from a boat than it does to fish from inside a Fish Trap.

Still, you can see the evolution of the Winter Fishing System when it comes to overcoming the problem of being cold. Ice anglers have been cold forever—or else they've been fishing out of a permanent shack that robs them of their mobility. Today, we can maintain and even enhance our mobility while staying warm and comfortable.

Warm and comfortable aren't exactly the same things, in my mind. It rains and sleets and we walk through slush while we're ice fishing. So our clothes and our shelters need to keep us both warm and dry. Dry means comfortable.

A Fish Trap has been compared to a bass boat on the ice, but these days, I think of it as even more than that, because bass boats don't offer walls that can be flipped up around you in a few seconds, that keep the wind and rain and snow off of you, and in fact enhance your ability to focus on your fishing by taking away outside distractions. These days, I think of the Fish

Today's ice clothing is light!

Trap as more than a boat for ice fishing—more like a climate-controlled, instantly mobile shelter that holds all your gear.

And yet, the Fish Trap is just one piece of the equipment we use to remain mobile on the ice. Our clothing doesn't look like traditional ice fishing garb any more. Our boots are lightweight, made for hiking as much as sitting still, lined with waterproofing material that keeps our feet dry. We wear the same boots we wear for hunting, in fact, and they're much sleeker than the boots most people think of as being for ice fishing.

Socks and long underwear are made from high-tech materials that transfer perspiration away from the skin, where it can evaporate rather than create that clammy, chilled feeling you get with traditional fabrics like cotton. And our outside layer is basically high-tech raingear, which blocks the wind and keeps us dry, yet maintains that ability to transfer perspiration away from the inside layers of our clothing and out where it can evaporate.

These days, lots of people remark that it doesn't look like we're dressed warmly enough for ice fishing. But we are. Remember, we fish an active style, where we're moving quickly from spot to spot until we catch fish. We aren't dressed to sit outside on a deer stand, we're dressed to move, move, move, drill holes, drill holes, drill holes, and fish inside a Fish Trap.

And now for a bit of controversy. We use small heaters inside the Fish Trap to stay warm. Manufacturers of small heaters don't like to go on record as endorsing their products for use in heating up small spaces like the inside of a fish house, because if the fish house is 'tight' enough, the heater quickly consumes oxygen and you run the real risk of passing out and being found dead. But we use them, because air circulates quite well under the side flaps of a Fish Trap, and we flip the top up often to keep fresh air inside.

We're uncomfortable coming right out and endorsing the use of heaters, too, because it's critical to understand the potential for danger. But heat is sweet when it's cold outside, and we use a heater to keep our fingers nimble enough to tie knots, and to stay warm when it's really cold.

We rig up all sorts of lighting contraptions, too, so we can fish right up until dark, and after dark. Winter is short on daylight, and you can be fishing bluegills until dusk, then switch to crappies for an hour after dark, and it's only 5:30 or 6 o'clock in the evening when you quit. Lights mean comfort, too, even if it's just for packing away your stuff at the end of the day.

Presentation Equipment

It's impossible to separate the importance of being mobile, comfortable, and then presenting a bait to a fish. They're all important. You can't catch a fish unless you first find one, and that's why we usually talk about mobility first. But you also can't catch a fish unless you present a bait to it—one that the fish is willing to bite.

Ice Rods

Today's ice fishing rods are made for ice fishing, and that's no small point. We finally have well-crafted rods, made from the right materials, created to handle the light line and light lures we use to tempt bluegills.

With the right ice rod—and thin line that hangs straight—you can feel a tiny ice jig like a Fat Boy as you jiggle it. This is critical, because a lot of times, it's the absence of the weight of the jig that lets you know you had a bite. Bluegills rarely create even a good 'tick' when they bite.

The right rod needs to be stiff enough to transmit feel, to help you detect bites and feel your presentation. Those noodle-like soft rods, the ones with the soft (wimpy) fiberglass tips, are often called 'sensitive,' but they absolutely are not! They mush up and down when you try to jiggle a bait, and the mushiness completely robs you of your sensitivity. You catch fish with rods like that despite your equipment, not because of it.

Within reason, stiffness equals sensitivity. Ice rods for panfish need to be designed as ice rods, with the tapers right so sensitivity is retained with a

Notice that today's modern ice rod bends "like an open-water rod in miniature." Made from solid graphite, with powerful butt sections and light tips, they are extremely sensitive and strong for their weight.

very light lure. They must exhibit the right power and flex—strength in the butt section, 'strong flexibility' in the tip—so as you fight a bluegill the rod stays bent. If your rod comes to 'rest' (straightens out) as you battle the fish, slack line is the result—which means the fish is in danger of getting off.

When you rig up right, the rod, reel, and line create a harmonious package that fishes bluegill jigs well. Choose the rod based on the line, and the average weight jigs you'll fish with it. You do *not* choose a rod based on the size fish you plan to catch!

I'm proud to have my name on a signature series of ice rods from Berkley. Two models are suited well to bluegill fishing—meaning they fish light panfish jigs well. Check out the 24-inch model, #LSIS24L-R; and the 28-inch version, #LSIS28L-R. Both are light-action rods, rated for 1- to 4-pound-test.

The Right Line

The rod can be perfect, but if you match it with line that's too heavy, an ice jig appropriate for bluegills can't make it hang straight. Coils or curls in the line mean you are not in direct contact with the jig as you fish. Even a minor problem in this area can make it almost impossible to feel a bluegill bite.

For ice fishing, you want a low-stretch line. Lines that are too limp are not good for ice fishing because they're too 'stretchy' to give you good feel and solid hooksets. Ask knowledgeable sales people at sporting goods stores to show you which lines are low in stretch, and choose one that's thin enough in diameter to allow the baits you use to hang straight.

A tiny ice fly won't make thick, stiff line hang straight, and that makes it difficult to get the lure to do what it should, and tougher to detect bites.

I personally like clear line, especially for daytime fishing. Any line that I can readily see, I have a hard time using, because I just don't have confidence in it.

I have used extremely thin, light line for panfish, down to less than 1-pound-test. But lately I've settled on thin-diameter 2-pound. My personal favorite is Berkley Micro Ice. In 2# test, it's .0053" diameter, same as Trilene XL. It's soft and pliable, with low-stretch properties, so it has good sensitivity and helps with solid hooksets.

Pay close attention to diameter. If a line breaks at 4 pounds of pull, it's not 2-pound-test, even if it says it is on the box. Remember, the lure you choose to fish with has to make your line hang straight down, tight. Any lure too light to make new, thin-diameter 2-pound line hang straight is probably too light to fish with.

(One potential problem presented by very light line: if you set the drag on your reel so fish can run, when the drag is slipping the line is twisting. It's difficult to set your drag for 2-pound-test and get a fish up the hole. So I tend to fish light line on a tight drag, and backreel to land a good fish.)

Reels

A variety of reels will work well, as long as they're not too big or heavy that they 'unbalance' the outfit. Get yourself a small spinning or closed-face 'underspin' reel that feels comfortable in your hand. I'm amazed at the number of ice anglers who still don't use a rod and reel. It's as if setting the hook by hand, dropping the rod in the snow, and hand-over-handing the fish is part of their DNA. Keeping equipment functional while you're on the ice is part of the game, and a lot of anglers still don't use a rod and reel because they can't throw it in the snow after every fish and still have it work.

Do they drop their rod in the sand or on the bottom of the boat in the summer when they set the hook on a fish, then hand-over-hand the line in? That way of fishing was created because of jiggle sticks, because small reels were not available. Now, we have better alternatives.

Jigs and Live Bait

The right jigs and the right bait are part of the System, too.

Everybody seems to have their preferences when it comes to ice jigs for bluegills. For me, at least on most days, it comes down to small jigs that 'fish heavy,' a term that I've been using for years now. Like the Fish Trap and Ice Box, they didn't exist, so I worked with System Tackle to create what we wanted. In my book, it's hard to beat the Fat Boy and smaller Genz Worm for bluegills. These jigs show up well on a flasher, they give you excellent feel when jigging, and they are 'horizontal' jigs, meaning they swim naturally—which is important, especially when you're trying to fool big 'gills when sight fishing in clear water.

You need fresh live bait to tip the jigs with for best results. My two favorites, hands-down, are colored larvae (maggies) and wax worms. You'll hear me say this elsewhere in this book, but don't try to see how many fish you can catch without re-baiting. The key to catching fish is location, location, location, fresh bait, fresh bait, fresh bait.

There's a right and wrong way to hook maggies and wax worms on your jig, which I'll detail in the next chapter on presentation.

Other things work well, too, such as soft plastics. Also, on reluctant

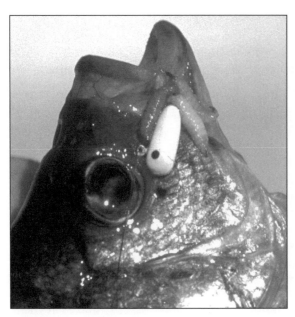

The Fat Boy, shown here, is an example of a horizontal ice jig that "fishes heavy" for its size. Tip it with multi-colored maggies for increased appeal to bluegills. Wax worms are another good choice. Check out the details on hooking live baits properly in our Presentation chapter.

Each time you reel up the jig, check the position of the knot in the eyelet. Slide the knot around, if necessary, so the jig hangs horizontally, and fishes horizontally.

biters we've had good success using a trailer hook of some sort (attached to the hook of an ice jig). These are virtually neutrally buoyant, and often fool fish that won't bite anything else. Some very good bluegill chasers use flies—more commonly fished in open water on a fly rod—and tiny plain hooks baited with live bait. At times, they tie the fly in above the ice jig, so it's not on a trailer at all, but just dangling there, a smaller tidbit with undulating hair.

I'm going to be brutally honest here: in the beginning of the ice fishing revolution, when we first started using depthfinders, if we saw fish beneath us, we were much more likely to sit over the top of them, even for hours at a time, and try to get them to bite. As we became more and more mobile, we started to call those fish 'sniffers,' and we've become much more likely to keep moving until we find biters.

There are some anglers who would rather try for sniffers than keep moving, because they find fun and challenge in it. Do whatever you like best, but experience has taught me that, to catch the most fish by the end of the day, keep moving and go after biters.

Sniffers beware! A tiny trailer hook, baited with a single maggie, can turn the trick on reluctant bluegills.

Depthfinder

As I mentioned, a flasher is my favorite type of depthfinder to use through the ice. I realize that the liquid crystal graph is considered state-of-the-art for use in a boat, but the flasher has compelling advantages in ice fishing.

The multi-color display and overall quality of performance make the Vexilar FL-8 my choice, and I've fished with every unit available. A flasher simply updates its signal faster than a liquid crystal does, so you get instantaneous feedback on what your jig is doing, and how fish are reacting to your presentation. You see fish come into your hole, you watch whether they continue to approach, sit there and look, or swim away in response to what you do. I've called the FL-8 a 'mood indicator,' and I still feel that way; it clues me in on how the fish want the bait on any given day.

Without one, you can't experiment meaningfully with your presentation. With one, ice fishing is very exciting. I've also compared ice fishing with a good flasher to playing a video game. Show me a teenager who doesn't like to play this game, with real live targets, and I'll show you a kid who doesn't like to have fun.

If you have a liquid crystal and just can't justify buying a flasher for ice fishing, by all means, take the graph with you. Just make sure you rig it up for ice fishing, in an Ice Box with a good gel-cell battery. The batteries nowadays are lightweight, work well in extremely cold temperatures, and there's no concern about getting battery acid on your clothes or equipment should the battery tip over.

Your FL-8 is your underwater vision. It's a huge part of the System.

Lake Maps

It still amazes me that most people wouldn't consider going out on the water without a lake map in the summer, but never take one with them in the winter. You'll be able to find sections of the lake that look promising, and even specific spots you want to check. We'll get into what spots to look for, based on water type, in future chapters. And on some waters, such as farm ponds, you don't need a contour map because you can just check the whole thing with a depthfinder in a reasonable amount of time.

Augers

Augers may have progressed as much as any part of our equipment. It wasn't too many years ago that it was hard work to drill more than a few holes. Now, with the Strikemaster Lazer augers we use (they're available in hand, electric, and gas power models), it's nothing to cut holes.

You can imagine how important a good, sharp auger that cuts through the ice with little effort is to your overall

Strikemaster Lazer augers, in electric (left) and gas (right) models, and the modern Lazer cutting blades (inset). They really are a better auger.

attack. I think of drilling holes as being similar to making casts in open water. The more 'casts' I can make, the more fish I'm likely to find, and catch. It just makes sense. Again, we don't wait for the fish to come to us. We take it to the fish, every time out.

Lately, though, I've seen excessive drilling become part of some anglers' approach. I have been guilty myself of pumping people up on this subject, I'm afraid, talking sometimes of how my partners and I "drilled a hundred holes" in a day's fishing. I've seen guys cut 50 holes, or even a hundred, in an area—before they drop a line down!

My approach is summed up like this: I fish in every hole I drill. I usually drill maybe three, or four, or five holes, then fish them. I don't drill a hundred holes in one general area. I normally check an area, drilling only enough holes to allow me to feel like I've made a reasonable effort to find fish (this varies, depending on how big and complex the area is).

If I don't find fish in one general area, it's common for me to move a ways before drilling again. At the end of the day, I may have drilled a hundred holes, if I add them all up. But I would say you don't need to run a tank of gas through your auger before you start fishing. You're out there to fish.

GPS

I love using hand-held Global Positioning System (GPS) units to save good spots I find, and return to them on future trips. If you've never used a GPS, or don't understand how they work, they are a navigational instrument that pins down your location on the earth by tracking satellites.

Because of government-introduced error (for military security), a GPS unit won't always get you back into your old set of footprints. But they generally work accurately enough to put you darn close—certainly close enough that you can pin down the spot by drilling a few holes and using your depthfinder. The cost of these units is coming down all the time (in the $200-300 range for a good one), something you should consider if your budget allows it.

The Mobile Mindset

When you collect all the pieces, and you're dressed in the right clothes, you are a machine ready to fish through the ice. I think you see now why we refer to it as the System—and why it takes a while when somebody asks me to explain what I mean by my 'System.'

Your equipment will allow you to remain warm and comfortable, and you will have everything you need sliding along behind you in the Fish Trap. You can check depths, and see fish. Your rod, reel, line and bait are a matched set.

In short, you are ready to be a modern ice angler. The only thing that can hold you back now is the old way of thinking. I've seen any number of people who, despite having all the right gear, still fish like they don't. They drill one hole and sit there in their Fish Trap and don't catch anything.

You need the mobility mindset. You need to hit the water with optimism, and a plan. Ask at the bait shop where people have been catching bluegills, at what depth, in what type of cover. Go ahead and join a group of other anglers, just to see what kind of fish they're on, and what type of spot they're fishing.

But use your lake map, and use your Lazer auger, and use your FL-8. Find other spots, and fish them on your own. Keep moving until you find the fish you're after. On many days, you're going to catch one or two fish out of a hole and have to move to catch more. That's just how it is a lot of times.

If you can drill one hole and catch everything you want, by all means do it. But call me when you get home, so I can come out and drill a hole right next to you the following day.

Wait around too long for the fish to come to you, and you might freeze right into the ice. You need the 'mobile mindset' and the right gear.

CHAPTER THREE

UNDERSTANDING THE WINTER SEASONS

My personal notion of what makes up the various periods of the ice fishing season is based on years of observation. After spending this many winters chasing bluegills, patterns emerge, defined periods within the entire ice season that you notice, apparently brought on by significant changes in the environment that in turn affect location and behavior of the fish.

You'll hear me say this numerous times, but this whole business of trying to identify stages of the ice season depends on how long and severe the winter is in your local area. In some places, you might only experience first-ice conditions—because ice forms, thickens enough for fishing for a few days, then melts away, the process perhaps repeating several times each winter.

But where winter hits hard, where fishable ice remains for months and snow cover becomes a factor most years, you see changes worth noting.

Here, then, is how I chart the changes, from a fishing perspective, from first ice through breakup.

Pre-Ice Scouting

This gets written up occasionally in fishing magazines, but it's probably the most universally-ignored facet of ice fishing. You need to start the winter fishing experience before the ice forms, during the weeks before ice-up, running around in your boat using a depthfinder and GPS (or using shore-sightings).

You want to find where the fish are, by fishing for them, and you want to study the condition of the weeds and check out the clarity of the water. Keep a record book if you can be disciplined enough, and you are building a huge set of shortcuts for after ice covers the lakes.

Find out where the weeds are still standing. In shallow water, weeds freeze into the ice, and can remain standing for the entire winter. When you can zip around in a boat and get a high-speed reading on a depthfinder, you can do a lot of work in a short period of time that would take much longer after the ice forms.

First Ice

Get out there as soon as it's safe to do so, but don't rush it. Read our chapter on ice safety to thoroughly familiarize yourself with what's safe and what's not. At this time, the bluegill bite can be good, and shallow weeds are always a good bet. But beware of the fall when the weather stays nice right up until ice. Bluegills, like other fish, can be stuck in early fall patterns and not where you would expect them at first ice.

Oxygen depletion is not a factor at this time. Now is probably the best time to fish smaller waters, like small natural lakes and ponds.

Decreased Light Penetration

I call this 'the cloudy period.' It's a transition time between first ice and midwinter. You can recognize this period by an increase in dying and dead weeds, and cloudy water.

The water might have been nice and clear earlier in the winter, but now it's cloudier. Some people say the water got 'all riled up.' Well, what riled it up? Ice is covering the surface, so there is no wind.

This period begins about the time we get 'driving ice' in Minnesota, and that's when we notice a change in the fishing. The ice is thicker, there's less light penetration, and usually snow cover. In your area, it might be just thicker ice and snow cover. Even in the fringe areas of the ice belt—where it can get warm enough to melt and thaw without losing all the ice—the ice is not clear after a while. Sometimes, it floods and refreezes and that makes it milky, and there's less light penetration.

Even without these external factors that limit light penetration, many underwater plants have annual cycles governed by day length. So it's actually the shortening daylight hours (photoperiod) that cause many weeds to just maintain what vigor they can, and sort of 'mark time' until spring. Still, this noticeable decrease in light penetration through the ice is probably the 'kicker' that causes certain weeds to brown up and start to decompose. When plants die off or when phytoplankton population growth declines, a feeding frenzy by decomposing bacteria follows. It becomes a cycle that causes dropping oxygen levels, as the population levels, and activity, among these 'primary decomposers' grows.

It's interesting that there are huge, and roughly equal, populations of decomposer bacteria in all lakes, regardless of how clear, dirty, fertile, or infertile the water. The differences become noticeable only based on how

many are active at any given time in any given body of water.

The scientists who study the workings of a lake under the ice speculate on various reasons for this clouding of the water. One likely cause: dead and dying algae and weed particles suspended in the water, being attacked and consumed by bacteria and fungi.

But there are other known causes.

Sometimes, phytoplankton deplete dissolved carbon dioxide levels to a point that a calcium carbonate precipitate is produced. This phenomenon is called "lake whitening" because the water takes on a milky appearance. Fine sediments suspended in the water can also produce a 'cloudiness,' and so can large numbers of microscopic organisms.

In addition to providing less protection to the bluegills from their natural predators, the shriveling, atrophied brown weeds deny bluegills access to some of the insects that are on them.

So it is the increase in activity level of decomposer bacteria (spurred by an increase in available dead and dying plants) that depletes oxygen levels. Oxygen levels can get too low for most fishes, and can be the reason bluegills vacate these shallow, weedy areas—places that may have housed good fishing in previous weeks.

Bottom line, in English: it's common to see bluegills move into deeper, cleaner, clearer water once the cloudy period sets in.

Midwinter

Fishing gets tougher. Bluegills are often in deeper, more oxygenated water. I think these fish, in a lot of waters, quit feeding for a time. I have a theory that it gets to a point where there just isn't much food in some lakes during the 'dead' of the midwinter period, and the fish go into a semi-hibernation state. They don't move, and they don't exert energy.

Where good fishing existed earlier in the winter, it can seem like no fish exist at all.

Being cold-blooded, it may be that the fish don't have to take in any food for a time as long as they remain dormant, a condition I've seen biologists refer to as a *torpor*. When their body temperature goes down, they don't die, but perhaps they sense there is very little food available to them and they enter something of a survival mode.

It's interesting that on some lakes, you just don't catch any fish at any point in the winter. Some lakes with darn good bluegill fishing in the summer produce nothing through the ice. Could it be that the major food sources on these lakes doesn't stay 'stocked' well enough after the ice forms to support feeding, so the bluegills basically 'hibernate' for lack of a better term? I wish I knew the answers.

I know this: generally, when I'm catching bluegills through the ice I always seem to have suspended particles on my depthfinder screen. You don't have a 'clean screen' when you're catching fish, and I'm constantly turning down the gain to minimize the interference. I think that's the food process, the cycle of life, going on under the ice. When it's absent, the fishing slows down, too.

What Do Winter Bluegills Eat?

Under the ice, what is available for bluegills to eat?

Bluegills eat a wide variety of food items, but a lot of the miniature 'animals' they consume are rare or nestled somewhere out of reach in winter. Regional, lake-to-lake, and even hour-to-hour variations occur, depending on what is available to bluegills on a local basis.

Aquatic insects—

Bluegills eat more aquatic insects than anything else, and midge larvae top the list. Unfortunately for 'gills, many midge larvae seal themselves in overwintering cocoons for the winter. This doesn't make them unavailable, just harder to find. There are, however, a lot of other aquatic insects active in the winter.

Zooplankton—

In general, zooplankton are rare in the water column during winter. The bigger the critter the better for 'gills. Daphnia are big 'zoops' that you can see at arm's length with the naked eye. Many daphnia retire to the lake bottom sediments for the winter while their food source (phytoplankton) is scarce. Copepods are around, but not in big numbers because they also eat phytoplankton and thrive in warmer water. Most rotifers wait winter out, too, as resting cysts and eggs, but there are some around.

Plants—

Bluegill guts, when studied, sometimes have vegetable matter in them, but nutritional value to a bluegill is not considered important.

This midwinter period is the time when larger lakes generally produce better than smaller ones. It's not the best time of year to fish a large lake, necessarily, but it can be the time to choose a large lake over a small one. But don't hit the large lake and go straight to where the crowd has been since first ice. Those fish have been tapped; they've gone home in buckets. Search out your own fish, at this time more than any other period.

One alternative strategy that I've been using in recent years is to chase the early-ice period by traveling to other states. Simply going south from my home base in Minnesota, I can get to early-ice conditions after the doldrums hit. Similarly, you can follow late-ice conditions north as they occur, as ice melts on the southern fringes of ice country.

Late Ice

Shiny wetness appears around a branch or leaf lying on the ice surface. Snow starts melting, creeks start running, water collects on top of the ice and runs back down your hole when you drill it.

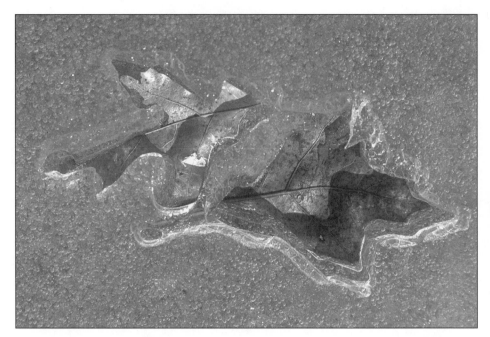

Runoff has begun, and the bluegills often return to the shallows that they vacated during the cloudy period or midwinter.

In shallow water, plants start growing again, in response to increasing daylength. They kick out oxygen during the daylight hours, which makes the shallows hospitable to bluegills again. Insects, also in response to the lengthening photoperiod, show an impressive increase in activity. That brings the bluegills in for the feeding opportunities.

At the beginning of this period, bluegills return to the weedlines, and by last ice, can be in the extreme shallows. In a nutshell, the shallow world is accessible to the fish again, and they move up to sometimes only a foot of water under the ice. They're feeding on insects and other food items that collect on reed stalks or other weeds or cover types.

Don't look for 'gills on shallow sand flats, though; confine your search to spots that would have lush vegetation in the summer. At this time, it's common to see weeds growing under the ice. An underwater camera can be a great tool, because the water can still be cloudy, but you can identify green weeds growing right among decaying weeds. The weed-growing shallows can be like a flower bed in spring, where all these dead plants are surrounded by the new sprouts pushing up through and competing for the sunlight. If you find this situation, it's a good bet the bluegills have found it, too.

This can be some of the best ice fishing for bluegills of the entire winter, but ice conditions can be dangerous. Again, read the ice safety chapter to brush up on the pitfalls of late ice, then carefully make your way out to some memorable angling. Just don't push it.

Know when to go home and get your boat ready for ice-out.

Chapter Four

Locating Bluegills
(How Clear is the Water, Momma?)

Water clarity and weeds are everything. Those are the two main factors when it comes to locating bluegills.

Clear or dirty. Weeds or no weeds. Standing, green weeds or dead weeds laying on the bottom.

Those *are* the lake types, when it comes to bluegills.

We have arrived at the most important aspect of catching bluegills through the ice... finding them.

The goal here is to make you a successful bluegill angler in any region of the ice belt, at all periods of the winter. I feel confident, at least most of the time, about making bluegills bite once I find them. Most days, if we see fish come into our holes when we're sight fishing, or mark them on our FL-8, they'll bite.

So the finding can be the hard part, and the prospect of striking off on your own can seem daunting. The security blanket of the crowd on the community spot can be hard to break away from. But trust me, the rewards of setting the hook into stubborn resistance when you're the only one on the spot are worth the effort.

Let's prepare you for becoming a fish hunter.

How clear is the water, momma?

At least when it comes to bluegills, the type of system they are found in is not a huge clue as to location. In the ice belt, 'gills are found in natural lakes, manmade reservoirs, rivers, ponds and pits. In my experience, bluegills are bluegills, and will tend to be in predictable places, regardless of the water type, based on what is available.

When it comes to finding bluegills, the number one thing—in any body of water—is water clarity.

When you're looking for 'gills, ask yourself about the color of the water. Check a map, ask at the bait shop, drill a hole and see for yourself.

How clear is it? Are there weeds, or not? If there are weeds, how deep do they grow?

Water clarity and weeds are everything. Those are the two main factors.

All bluegill-holding waters can be broken into clear water, dirty water, or somewhere in between water. If the water is dirty, there may be weeds, but only in the shallows because sunlight doesn't penetrate and allow deeper plant growth. If the water is clear, there might be weeds that grow quite deep. In any fishery that has weeds, those weeds might be standing upright, laying on the bottom, or a combination of both.

When it comes to bluegills, those are the lake types.

Lakes, ponds, pits, and backwaters of reservoirs and rivers, all fall into one of these 'categories.' Also, based on the length and severity of winter, any given body of water might change in these important physical features from one period of the winter to another. In other words, there might be an abundance of healthy, standing weeds at early ice, but by midwinter, most of the weeds may be laying on the bottom—heavy snow cover and resulting loss of light penetration having robbed the plants of their vitality.

These are the main factors that affect bluegill location.

Water clarity is going to dictate whether the fish are shallow or deep. In real clear water, you can have fish in 15 feet of water living in the weeds. In other systems, 15 feet can be the deepest water, and the water might be quite discolored, with very little weed growth at any depth. There are various stages between these extremes.

And the type of weeds can make a difference. Cabbage and coontail are two of my favorites. Junk weeds are usually not standing weeds in winter under the ice. An area might be 'weed-choked' in the summer, but a barren flat in the winter because all the weeds are dead and laying down. The weeds have to be up, at least somewhat, for them to offer protection from predators.

In some lakes, where the weeds all fall down later in the winter, if you have clumps of reeds—you'll often see them sticking up through the ice—bluegills will use them, too.

At seminars, I'm often asked by people who are going to fish a strange lake how they can find the bluegills. I ask them the following questions:
- How deep do the weeds grow?
- Do the weeds stay green all winter?
- Are the weeds dead or alive?

It's critical to realize that a lake can make a transition in the middle of the winter, say from clear to dirty. Snow cover can cause weeds to die, and that can cloud up the water, and now this is a whole new lake from what it was just a few weeks before! Late in the ice season, melt-water can run back into the lake and dirty it up.

One thing I hear from people is "one year, we caught them over here, but we never caught 'em there again." Well, it has to have something to do with weeds or water clarity, or both.

Was it a hot or cool summer? How healthy were the weeds in the fall? You get a good, hot summer, that can affect the winter. If a lake turns pea green in the summer (they don't all do this) and all the weeds go down because of lack of light penetration, how healthy do you think those weeds are going to be come winter? Sometimes, fertilizer or other manmade compounds can influence this, too.

The bottom line is: how clear is the water, and are there any weeds?

Like many things in life, it's as simple, and as complex, as that.

Other Considerations

- The size of the fishery is important. In the case of ponds and pits, for example, location can be simple, because they're generally small. It might take just an hour or so to determine where the fish are holding, because you can easily walk around drilling holes in every possible spot. A big lake, or expansive backwaters in reservoirs and river systems, require a more systematic search strategy.
- The relative size of a fishery based on where it is, geographically, is also important. In regions that feature long winters and heavy snowfall, smaller ponds, lakes and river backwaters tend to produce better fishing early and late in the season, and can be difficult to catch fish out of in the middle of

On Becoming a Fish Finder

To become a fish finder, you have to make judgements about the water you're on. When it comes to bluegills through the ice, a lot of my judgements are based on how clear the water is, and how deep the weeds grow.

You can't say water clarity and weeds are always the only thing influencing where you find good bluegills: I've caught them, for example, on deep flats outside the weedline, if the bottom composition is right and food is available. But it's the best starting point, that's for sure.

Experience counts for a lot. Lack of time ice fishing makes it hard for many people to have confidence in deciding where to try, and where to move next if that doesn't work. At least you're starting with a lot of information I never had when I started out. You might not be successful the first time you go to a lake, but you'll learn something. You should catch something, and get closer to figuring out where the nice fish must be.

Making choices is a big part of fishing. Guessing what to do that might be right. If they're not here, where are they? You don't say they're not biting. You do get to that on some days, but more times than not, if you can locate bluegills you can make them bite.

Don't forget your lake map.

the ice-over period. It's probably an oxygen thing. By comparison, a larger lake would probably be a better choice in the middle of the ice season.

• High and low water cycles are important to track. All systems go through periods of relatively lower and higher water levels. During periods of high water, the system tends to have more food per fish, and this seems to allow the bluegills to get bigger than they otherwise would. I love high-water cycles. High water can change fish location, too. For example, let's say a bay normally has about 3 feet of water in it. Bluegills will vacate such a spot before the ice even forms, and won't be there all winter, assuming deeper water is available. But if that bay suddenly has 8 feet of water in it, the 'gills might be able to winter in there.

• You need to know that a given system has good bluegills in it. Don't fish there if there isn't a good bluegill population. Reports created by your local biologists are more available than ever, either by contacting their office or searching the internet. And many of today's contour lake maps include test-netting data, noting size and abundance of the fish species found in the body of water.

An Interview With Dave Genz
On Locating Bluegills

This is your editor speaking. I hope you agree that when great anglers answer questions it makes fascinating reading. Dave Genz is a great interview, because he thinks before he answers even the most basic question.

Here's Dave Genz on various aspects of finding bluegills.

Q: *You've pointed out the most obvious and what you consider the most critical things to consider when searching for bluegills. First, the system has to have a good population of decent 'gills. Next, you look at water clarity, presence or absence of weeds, and what condition the weeds are in. But what are some other important considerations?*

Dave: Bottom content is another key. Bluegills are not on goopy, silted, muddy bottom most of the time. And if the bottom is too hard, like hard sand or packed clay or gravel or rock, that's normally not a good bluegill spot, either. Too hard is not good, and too soft is not good, either.

You can learn a lot by taking a lead weight—those heavy snap-on sinkers we used to use to set the depth of our bobber rigs—and pounding it on the bottom. If it just kind of sticks a bit, but you can pop it free, that's the kind of bottom where weeds can grow. When it hits hard sand, you know you aren't going to find thick cabbage weed there. You fish bluegills where the bottom is right for weeds and bugs.

That isn't to say you never find 'gills over mucky bottom. In deeper water, you can have them suspended up off the bottom. If you're talking weed fish, the bottom has to be right.

Bluegill location is all relative to food. No matter what type of water they're in, they have to be where food is. If there's no food, they might go into a semi-dormant state, sort of shut down. I think that happens sometimes, when bluegills eat down their natural food supply in the winter. We always blame it on low oxygen, but is it always? I don't know for sure, but I have my theories. Why do bears hibernate in the winter? Because there's nothing for them to eat. Generally, the fish that are hard to catch, their stomachs are empty. When the bite's tough, and you manage to catch a fish, you open them up and their bellies are empty. They're never stuffed.

Q: *You talk about weeds a lot. How important, if you could summarize it into one statement, are weeds when it comes to locating bluegills?*

Dave: Generally, if you have weeds that are standing and green, fish the weeds. To know for sure what we've got, we need to know the weedline. How deep do the weeds grow? If the weeds grow about 8 feet or deeper, that's generally a clear lake and bluegills relate to the weeds. If the weedline is in less than 8 feet, the weeds tend to fall down in the winter under the ice cover and fish relate to deep water. That's not always true, but it's a rule of thumb.

There are some lakes where the maximum depth is only 10 feet, and bluegills live in the weeds all winter in 3-4 feet of water. There are exceptions, but no matter what, you're still looking for the best weeds.

Some good strong weeds can grow near the surface in the summer and actually freeze into the ice. The ice holds them in the 'up' position. They still might turn brown and die, but they can't fall down. They're usually in shallow water, which can often be low on oxygen in the midwinter. But when the fish come back into the shallows at late ice, those brown weeds, still standing because they're frozen into the ice, can be good cover for fish.

A lot of people probably don't realize that you can have weeds growing under the ice. If the ice is clear enough to allow for sunlight to get through, you can actually get new growth. I've seen new weeds growing under the ice at the end of January.

But when the weeds are brown and down, the weeds don't normally hold fish and they relate to the deeper water. Again, weeds can be standing and green at early ice, then snow cover can cut the light penetration, the weeds can die and lay on the bottom, and the bluegills move out to deeper water.

Not all regions will get enough snow to stay on the ice. In some places, you only have a few days or weeks of safe ice, so it stays early ice all the time. But in places where snow accumulates, that can be a sign that the shallows are becoming oxygen-poor. If you're having trouble getting around on the ice because of snow depth, that can be a clue that the fish are using deeper water. Under those conditions, if you're on a lake with both shallow weeds and deeper depressions, look in the depressions.

Q: *Is it true, all things being equal, that you'd rather find bluegills in shallow water than deep?*

Dave: For being efficient, yes, because you can get your lure down quicker in shallow water, and you can use a lighter jig if it doesn't have to fall so far. But I still believe, in most areas, if you can find deep-water 'gills they'll be the biggest ones in the lake. Sometimes they don't exist. Sometimes you only catch them on the inside of the weedline.

There's no deep-water bite on Lake Okoboji in Iowa, for instance. All the good bluegills are in the shallow weeds. But I'll give you another example from fishing in Michigan. I can easily say that when we fished in lakes that had good weed bites, in shallow water, the bluegills were noticeably smaller than when we went to lakes that had fish in 20 feet of water.

I think a lot of people get stuck in a rut when it comes to depth. I see guys who are shallow-water fishermen, who have developed a system that employs something very light, like a fly. They don't adjust and fish the deep-water fish, even on the same lake.

Q: *You say that deep-water bluegills are often the biggest ones in the lake. But how do you locate deep-water bluegills, especially on expansive deep flats or over basins?*

Dave: Oh, man. Where do I start? I'll try, although trying to describe all the possible deep-water spots that might hold bluegills in the winter isn't going to be easy. For one thing, it's breaks, dropoffs, whatever you want to call them, that don't echo on your depthfinder. That means they're not rock, or gravel, or even hard sand. Bluegills aren't on those types of bottoms.

The break can be kind of steep. In fact, I have this picture of what I think it must be like for bluegills to feed, and you could see how they'd do well if they're picking stuff 'off the wall' of a break, as compared to tipping down with their mouth to feed off the bottom. If you have one of those heavy clip-on weights we all used to use to check depths, hook it on your line to test the bottom composition. If it sort of sticks in the bottom, then you can pull it out, that's what you're looking for. You don't want it too hard or too soft.

This is the area where a lot of critters live, the stuff that bluegills eat. Nothing lives on a hard-sand break, probably because the bugs and larvae can't burrow into it.

The softest bottom, the muck, the ooze, is found in the basin. But on the bottom in the basin is not where you find bluegills. I don't think they can feed well off muck bottom.

When I'm looking for a possible deep-water bluegill spot, I study the lake map. Where the contour lines in the mid-depths, say 25 to 30 feet, are far apart, that means you have a 'shelf' between 25 and 30. Those areas seem to be right for bluegills, although you don't know for sure until you drill some holes and fish.

These are deep-water flats, in essence, even though they are probably technically part of the dropoff. And the bluegills in these areas tend to be a bit off the bottom, maybe 2-3 feet. They must be zooplankton feeders. You see masses of young-of-the-year panfish suspended in these areas, too, so they must be feeding on the same food source as the adult fish.

I also look for obvious holes surrounded by shallow water. On a lot of lakes, you have this huge stretch of shallow water, where weeds grow all summer, and then there's this hole, where the water might be 20 or 25 or even 30 feet deep.

One thing to watch for is a bay that's pretty isolated from the rest of the lake. Even if the bay seems to have sufficient depth, and the right bottom composition, it might not hold bluegills in the winter if it's in an area that has a long winter. Fish have an instinct for getting away from places they might get trapped in if the water levels drop or oxygen gets low. They tend to migrate out of bays that are isolated from the main part of the lake by a tight opening.

So it's holes surrounded by shallow water, and those shelves that have the right bottom composition. When you're talking deep-water bluegills, they're not weed fish.

Q: *As you search for bluegills, how often is an exact depth the key to catching them? In other words, do you sometimes find them in 12 feet, and 10 or 14 feet would be a bust?*

Dave: Sometimes, it's the makeup of the surrounding terrain that regulates where bluegills are, or where they go when they move. Fish don't usually move from one end of the lake to the other, but from one piece of structure to another, or maybe just down the weed edge a little ways. I've seen fish drop down deeper as a day unfolds, as the sun gets up in the sky and things get brighter. You can see big changes from a cloudy day to a clear day. I think it regulates the depth at which plankton—and the fish that feed on them—suspend. I believe the food sources, and even the bluegills, suspend at a depth level that makes them hard to see. If they're in shallow weeds, they can use the weeds for cover from predators. But if they're not in the weeds, they use shadows and low light levels—depth, in other words—as their cover.

Assuming the bottom is not pitch black, you can actually have more light at the bottom than a ways off bottom, because light seems to reflect off the bottom. I've definitely noticed that by using an Aqua-Vu camera.

I've seen the depth of the productive bluegill bite change while I'm out there, and I believe it has to do with light levels. In general, expect bluegills to go deeper under bright conditions, and shallower under more cloudy conditions.

But to answer the question, yes, bluegills seem to be either deep or shallow. It's one of those two things. They might be at 18 feet, and you'll find them at 18 feet all over the lake. That doesn't mean it's going to be like that forever, though. You have to stay flexible, and go back into search mode if your old way stops producing.

Q: *If finding weeds is such a key, but you can't see the weeds due to low light or dirty water, how do you know when you're over weeds?*

Dave: By using your depthfinder or an underwater camera. On an FL-8, weeds show up on the display as thin, weak signals, usually green or orange. It depends on how high you have the gain turned up and how deep the water is, but if you adjust your gain so that your ice jig shows up as a green or orange line, the weeds will, too. Sometimes, the weeds are thick from top to bottom, and that can tell you to drill some holes around the area to look for clearer pockets to fish in. It can be tough to get a jig down into lush weed growth and catch a fish before you snag up.

Q: *Just to get us pointed in the right direction, can you give us a summary of general bluegill movements through the winter season? Such as: they tend to be in such-and-such a place at first ice, then they move to such-and-such a spot later in the winter, stuff like that?*

Dave: It's tough to make general statements about bluegill location. What lake are you going to? Every fishery is going to be different. Again, it comes down to finding out how clear the water is, and what the weed situation is. So much depends on the period of the ice season, whether the lake is found in Wisconsin, where the ice comes on in November and stays until March, or Indiana, where the ice might only cover the lake for a few weeks.

For instance, at first ice, in the Mississippi River backwaters, I'm probably going to fish in 3 feet of water, because the fish live in shallow bays back there. In a farm pond, I'm going to start at the dam and work to the break. In one little lake that's a favorite of mine in Minnesota, I'm going to fish at 20 feet or deeper, even at first ice, because I know that's where the fish in that lake tend to be. But on a larger lake in another part of the state, I'm going to start in about 12 feet of water, in the weeds. It depends on what the lake has.

Q: *So when you see these general descriptions of bluegill movements through the seasons?*

Dave: If somebody is making statements, he's talking about one lake. A clear-water lake will function differently than a dirty-water lake, even if they're right across the road from each other. A dirty-water lake that has a lot of deep holes will function differently than a dirty-water lake with very little deep water.

If I'm choosing a lake, I like to go to a dirty-water lake where the 'gills are in deeper water. If I can find them in 18-20 feet, I can usually make them bite all day. These lakes don't have much for weed growth, so they tend to have good numbers of bluegills in deeper water.

Q: *So the key to learning to find your own bluegills is?*

Dave: It's a constant thought process when you're on the lake. You need to decipher the information you've got, and think about what's going on. You need to think like a tournament fisherman. Have a plan and execute the plan.

So many people get to the water and they stop thinking. They go back to doing what they always do, the one method they've been successful with the most. You need to try it shallow, and try it deep. Find the weeds, and punch holes in the weeds and fish them. Find out if the fish are in the weeds or not. If they're not in the weeds, they have to be somewhere else. If they're not shallow, they must be deep. You have to think, and eliminate things until you hit the right spots.

And you have to learn that it's not the magic lure thing. Sometimes, you need to go out when the fish are biting and try to find something you can't catch fish on. There's nothing magical about the bait when fish are biting. So many people think they're only catching 'em because they're using a green thingamajig.

Again, it's find the fish and you can usually make them bite. If you can't make fish bite, keep moving until you find some cooperative ones.

Q: *So should we give up trying to generalize about bluegill movements through the season?*

Dave: In a lot of cases, it's true that they start out shallow, in the weeds, then get forced into deeper water due to oxygen depletion. But that's only true in lakes that have weeds to hold the fish shallow early, and only where the winter is long enough to create oxygen problems. And only during years when there's enough snow cover, long enough, to create oxygen problems. Shallow shorelines are a dead sea in the middle of the winter on many lakes, but not all lakes. Do you see how hard it is to generalize?

It's always relative to food. Something's going on in nature at every season, drawing the fish to it. A lot of times, bluegills go deep in the midwinter period, and feed off bloodworms and other food sources in the mud. I never have caught bluegills in the summertime on the bottom in deep water, but you might find them suspended over deep water. But in the winter, bluegills are commonly in the basin of the lake. In the spring, those same fish come shallow again at late ice or once the ice goes away.

But again, remember that in a lot of places, you only get ice for a short period, so oxygen depletion is not a factor. It still comes down, pretty much every time, to water clarity and weeds.

You learn certain things about specific lakes that can help you in lakes that are similar. Let's use the shallow prairie lakes of Nebraska as an example. Most years, you have weeds almost everywhere—so at the beginning of the season, you're looking for pockets in the weeds so you can fish. It's hard to get your line down, there are so many weeds.

As the winter progresses and a lot of the weeds die and fall down, you end up looking for weeds that are still standing, so the fish have something to relate to, someplace to hide from predators. But that's a normal year. What if we get a year where the weeds don't grow as well in the summer? Then things would change even on those lakes. Sometimes reeds become the cover bluegills use to evade predators, so you catch them there. You have to think while you're out there. Look at what the conditions are.

Locating Bluegills: The Big Picture

Bluegills live in a wide variety of waters, but there are more similarities than differences in where the fish are found, regardless of what type of water you are fishing. To help you become better at locating bluegills, we've created maps of some of the highest-percentage spots.

You might find one or more of these spots on any given body of water—be it a natural lake, pond, pit, or backwater area of a river or manmade reservoir. Learn to recognize the characteristics of these spots, and you're way ahead of the pack when it comes to hunting down bluegills.

We've made depth markings on the contour lines of these maps, but don't think that these are the only depths that such spots will have. They are typical depths, known to hold bluegills, but the actual depth of any given dropoff, or flat, or inside turn, will vary.

Also, we make no claim that these are the only possible bluegill locations on all known bodies of water. You may have hotspots on your local lakes that are not represented here. It's difficult to generalize about spots, and fish location, because you always have the variables, such as water clarity, presence or absence of weeds, and severity of winter. It is up to you to test each type of spot, on your local waters, throughout the iced-over season. That way, you'll learn what your fish do. If you read the rest of this chapter and understand the basics of finding bluegills, you'll be able to succeed no matter where you fish.

The Big Picture

The universal truths when it comes to finding bluegills:

• Water clarity is the most important factor affecting bluegill location in any system. Clarity helps determine whether weeds are present in the body of water, and how deep the weeds grow.

• Generally speaking, in clear water where you have green standing weeds under the ice, you should fish in and around those weeds when searching for bluegills. In dirtier-water systems, weeds usually don't grow in deeper water, so they become less attractive to bluegills. Depending on how dirty the water is, weeds might not even grow well in shallow water.

• In northern climates where winter is long and snow often covers the lakes, oxygen depletion in the shallows often chases bluegills into deeper water as the winter wears on, even if they were found shallow at early ice.

• Where 'winters are long,' smaller waters such as ponds and small natural lakes tend to produce best at early ice and again at late ice, due again to oxygen depletion in midwinter. In such regions, it's often wise to fish smaller bodies of water early in the year, and fish larger systems at midwinter, after the bite on the smaller waters slows.

• Sometimes, you fish a spot that appears to have everything going for it, and catch nothing, or only small bluegills. Give a spot several tries before giving up on it. Also, you have to ask yourself whether the spot is 'private or pounded.' If a spot gets fished hard by a steady stream of people, it might produce nothing but small fish after a while, assuming many of the fish are kept.

• The truth is that not all lakes are good bluegill lakes. Face it, some lakes are crappie lakes, or perch lakes. Very few lakes raise adult fish of every species that they contain. Some don't have the right makeup to raise bigger bluegills. Some lakes can have small bluegills, but almost none that you would be interested in catching. We say this elsewhere in this book, and it may seem obvious, but a body of water needs to have a good bluegill population, and the potential to grow big bluegills, before you will catch big bluegills.

Inside Turns

Classic inside turns are a good bluegill bet. What's an inside turn? It's where deep water sort of 'carves a trough' into an area of shallow water (the deep water 'dips' into a shallow area), and you end up with 'walls' on three sides.

I have a theory that wind and waves through the fall weaken the strength of weeds on flats and points. These exposed and battered weeds then tend to die off and fall to the lake bottom earlier in the winter than weeds tucked into the shelter of inside turns.

On some lakes it's rarely an issue, because all the weeds seem to stand up all the time; but on other lakes, you might find the weeds on the flats and points laying on the bottom. Then, check the inside turns that might have weed growth in them. A lot of times, those weeds are healthy and standing, and can hold a lot of bluegills.

Another structural feature similar to an inside turn is something I like to call a 'corner.' Corners can occur along a shoreline break or a depression in a flat, and can be key areas for bluegills. A corner is like an inside turn, but less distinct. There are only 'walls' on two sides, you might say, instead of three.

Fish like to back up into inside turns and corners, so it's worth the effort find them. You can locate them easily if you can read through the ice with your depthfinder. If snow cover or cloudy ice makes it impossible to read through the ice, you'll have to drill enough holes to get an idea of where the corners and inside turns are.

Notice in our example that the back end of the inside turn occurs between about 10 and 15 feet deep. Weeds can grow in the inside turn, assuming the water is fairly clear, and the weedline in the lake is at least 10 feet deep. If the weedline is at 8 feet, there won't be any weeds in the inside turn. Bluegills can still be in the inside turn even if there aren't any weeds, because it's a fish-attracting feature regardless of how much cover is present.

If green weeds are standing on the wide spot in the dropoff between 10 and 15 feet, that zone can also hold bluegills. That's always a key question in any lake, at any point in the winter, when you're searching for bluegills. Are there nice weeds? At what depth are they growing? Some lakes have nice weeds all winter, or nice weeds all winter on some years.

When weeds die, bluegills usually move out of the weeds. An inside turn or corner can attract bluegills whether it has healthy weeds in it or not.

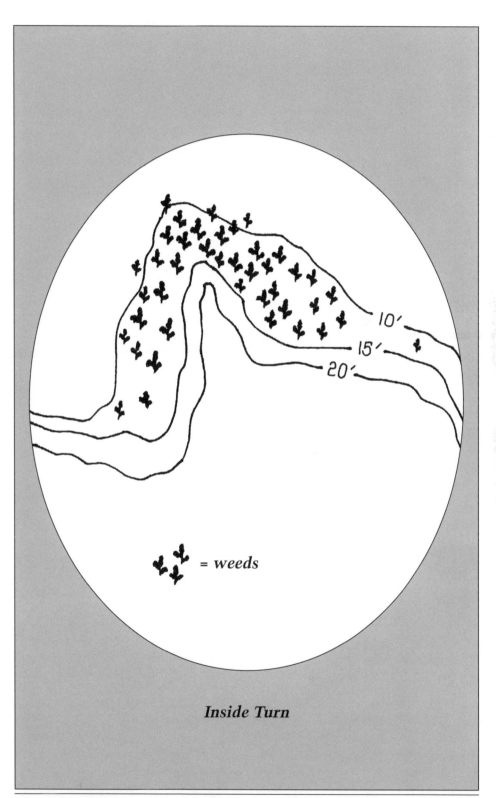

10'

15'

20'

= weeds

Inside Turn

'Multi-Featured' Spots

Here is a composite of numerous spots known to consistently hold good 'gills.

At first ice, I'd check the 8-10 foot levels for standing green weeds. Pay special attention to the 'corners' of the hole. Midwinter, if the green weeds have died off, check the deeper water in the hole (about 15-18 feet in this example). Late season, look for gills in 8 feet and shallower in the old weeds, especially clumps of old weeds. Fish often relate to dead weed patches late in the ice season, after the shallows are re-oxygenated.

Also look in the reed beds in late season. Reeds are under-fished hotspots at late ice.

Pay special attention to the points on the reed beds, which are normally easy to find because reed tops often stick up above the ice. If possible, find places where other varieties of weeds are growing among the reeds, or up to the edge of the reeds.

Interesting observation: Lakes that have large reed beds often grow big bluegills. It might be because they provide a wider variety of food sources for bluegills, ensuring consistent growth for the fish. If I have my choice between two lakes, and one has more reeds in it, I'll always choose to fish the one with more reeds.

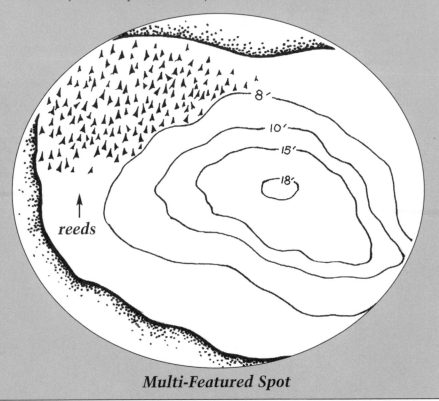

Multi-Featured Spot

Bluegills!

Narrows

Narrows are natural funnels, and they create current. They can hold bluegills on any body of water.

Current delivers food to fish. If you have a narrows in a lake, it's almost an automatic bluegill spot, especially at first ice.

Some narrows areas are obvious on a lake map, because they are necked-down passages where the opposite shorelines come close together. Less obvious spots are 'underwater narrows,' which can occur far from shore. Look on contour maps for places where where two shallower structural features create a long, thin deeper-water funnel, such as between a bar and a point.

How do you find bluegills in a narrows area? Just start drilling holes. You're looking for any features (weeds, other cover such as brush, depressions, humps) that might exist in the narrows. What makes a good narrows? There needs to be adequate depth to hold fish—which is always relative to how deep the rest of the system is.

Caution: thin ice is always a possibility anytime you have a narrows area.

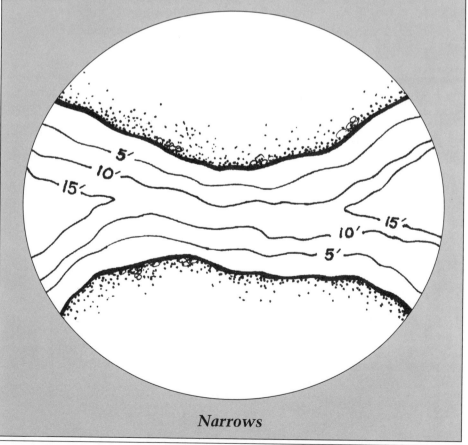

Narrows

Deep water 'sticky bottom' flats

Bluegill anglers are notoriously oriented toward 'weedline and shallower' depths. It can take some faith to target deep-water bluegills. I've said this before, but if you find deep-water bluegills, they tend to be the biggest bluegills in the system.

What is this spot? I call it a deep water, sticky bottom flat.

When you study a contour map, you're looking for places where the contour lines are relatively far apart, indicating a 'flat' between two dropoff areas. If the flat is shallow enough, and the water clear enough, you might have weeds growing on the flat. But at the mid-depths—deeper than weeds typically grow—you can have flats that house lots of life such as burrowing insect larvae.

The key is the bottom consistency.

I've described the bottom consistency you're looking for elsewhere in this chapter. One way to know it when you see it: at a gain setting adequate to display your ice jig on an FL-8, you don't get a second echo of the bottom. It's not soft and mushy, but it's not hard like rock or gravel, either. Another way to know it: clip a heavy weight onto your jig and lower it to bottom. If it 'thunks' hard, you know the bottom is too firm. If it mushes into oozing organic material, the bottom is too soft. If it sticks temporarily, and your rod tip flexes before pulling the weight free, it could be just right.

This is not the type of spot winter bluegill chasers are used to looking for, but it's well worth finding. It won't produce in all bodies of water, though; if you have a lot of shallow weed-oriented bluegills in a system, the deep-water sticky flats might not have fish on them. (Perch seem to 'own' this spot in lakes with shallow weed bluegills.)

In our example here, you'll notice that we've included a good stand of healthy cabbage weed. That's primarily to show how the two depth ranges are related, generally speaking. Again, if the lake has good weeds, check the weeds first. If there are few weeds, the sticky bottom flats can be a key attraction for bluegills.

If good stands of weeds exist at early ice, and produce bluegills, it's up to you to notice if the weeds die off at midwinter. If that's the case, bluegills might vacate the shallow weeds and head for the deep water sticky bottom flats.

In the real world, generally speaking, it's uncommon to have nice thick weed growth and a sticky-bottom deep-water flat just off of it. On any given spot, it's more common to have one or the other.

How do you pinpoint the location of bluegills on a deep water sticky bottom flat? Their exact location will change based on whether they're feeding on stuff that's burrowing into the bottom, or plankton and other matter suspended in the water column.

Assuming they're feeding on the bottom, bluegills can and do feed against the base of the slope—it's probably easier for them to feed 'against the wall' than directly off the bottom. Other bluegills will be scattered on the shelf, often suspended off bottom. You can also find bluegills, and crappies, suspended at the depth of the sticky-bottom shelf, but out over the deeper basin.

Many times, thankfully, these flats are not huge. And if they hold bluegills, they tend to be scattered all over it. It is often easy to drill holes all over such a spot (we call that 'drilling it out').

One challenge you can encounter is a massive number of young-of-the-year (YOY) bluegills. These fish can be the size of your thumbnail. They can be frustrating, because you might see a solid band of orange or red on your FL-8, and think you're seeing big fish. But study the depthfinder closely and you'll notice the signals are fading in and out, a clue that you're in one of these clouds of tiny 'gills. These fish often try to bite, and you think you're missing bites, but they're just too small to get hooked.

When you encounter this situation, take heart in the knowledge that, in a lot of cases, the bigger bluegills are below this band of YOY fish, or off to the side of it. Drill holes until you get away from the tiny fish and you increase your odds of catching a big fish.

To help you recognize this type of spot, we've included an overhead view of the same example, on the next page.

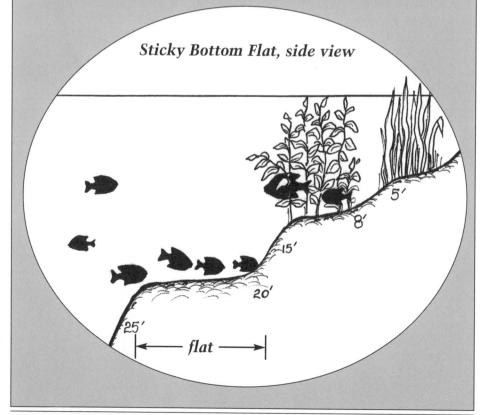

Sticky Bottom Flat, side view

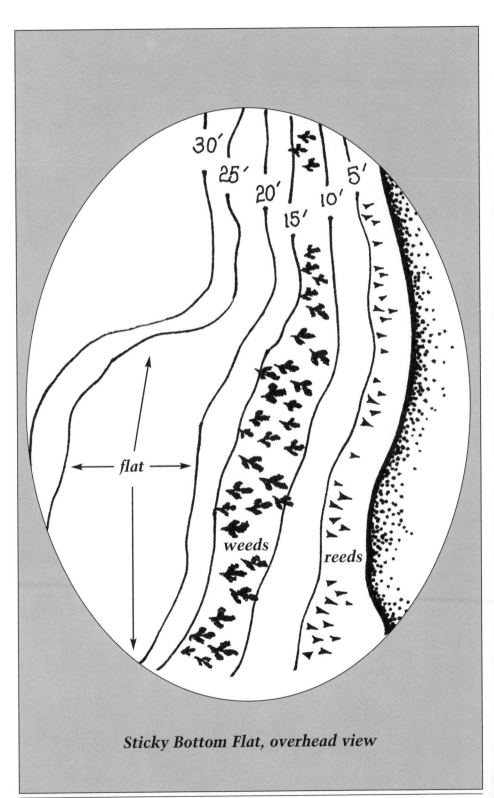

Sticky Bottom Flat, overhead view

Bluegills!

Deep water 'sticky bottom' flat

Overhead View

This is what a typical "deep water sticky bottom flat" would look like on a lake map (except that the symbols showing you where weeds and reeds are growing are not normally on a lake map).

Train your eye to notice spots like this, where the mid-depth contour lines are relatively far apart. In this case, again, it's the depth lines for 20 and 25 feet that are far apart. Contour lines spread apart like this indicate a gradually-sloping area, or 'flat.'

Part one of the puzzle is to find the flat. Part two, and the most important part: what is the bottom content? Once again, if the bottom content is right, the flat can hold lots of burrowing insect life that bluegills feed on.

Shallow and seemingly featureless areas

When you're faced with vast stretches of shallow water with few obvious structural elements, how do you find bluegills?

Entire lakes and ponds, or large sections of backwaters, can be like this. At first glance, many of these areas can seem too shallow to house bluegills throughout the ice season. In regions with long, harsh winters, that can be true; nature has taught bluegills to vacate large areas that are only 4 feet deep, if oxygen is going to become a problem at midwinter. But in many other instances, especially where the winter is shorter and less severe, current can keep the water oxygenated.

Also at first glance, it might seem there isn't a nickel's worth of difference in the depth, bottom content, or anything else. The answer is to look for features that may not be obvious from the study of a contour map. After you spend some time on the water, you might find, for example, sections of good weed growth, patches of underwater brush, or banks of reeds. There can often be 'holes,' too, spots where the water is deeper—if only slightly—than the surroundings. Long stretches of water might be uniformly 5 feet deep, then you come upon a 7- or 10-foot hole.

Early in the season you might have lush weed growth throughout these shallow areas, which can serve to scatter bluegills. In those cases, you're looking for pockets (openings) in the weeds. Bluegills often group up and feed in the openings. So there are a lot of fish in the pockets, plus it's easier to fish than in the thick of the weeds.

As the winter progresses, weeds can die off—even if current keeps the water oxygenated—as the ice gets cloudy or covered with snow, reducing sunlight penetration. That's when any slightly deeper depressions can be a real drawing card for bluegills. (In addition to the extra depth and 'side walls' that depressions provide to bluegills looking for cover, weeds often remain standing in them after weeds on the flats have died and fallen down.)

You might find 'humps,' too, spots where the water is a bit shallower than the surroundings. The bottom is usually firmer on the hump, and can support the healthiest weeds in the area. Patches of reeds can grow on humps, too.

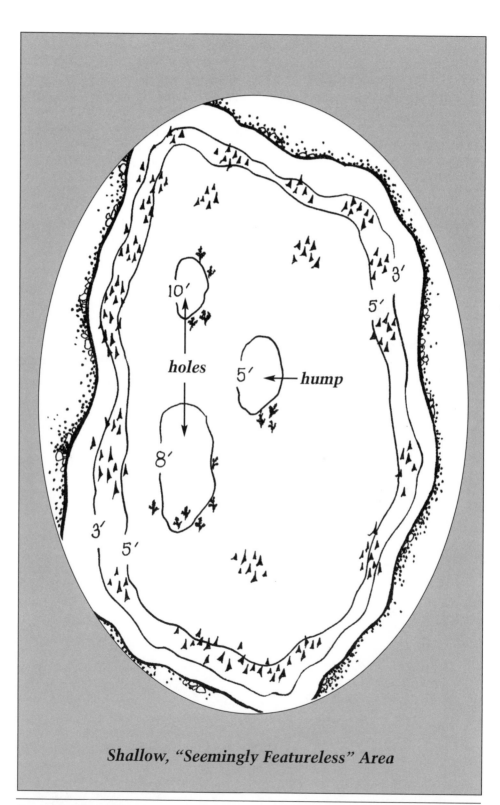

Shallow, "Seemingly Featureless" Area

A word about Ponds

In cattle country, they're called stock dams. In farm country, farm ponds, or just ponds. Whatever you call them, they can be great producers of big bluegills, especially if they don't receive much fishing pressure or if most of the big ones get released.

Typically, many anglers concentrate their efforts in the relative shallows of the ponds. I always go to the deepest water in the pond, and look with my depthfinder for bottom-hugging or suspended bluegills.

We always seem to end up spending most of our time in the deepest water. It's pretty much as simple as that. It's a relatively easy job to 'drill out' a pond. Sometimes, cover like sunken trees or brush piles can concentrate bluegills (and bass), all year. A little bitty tree near shore is no big deal, but a lot of times people sink brush into the deep water, and that can be the key spot.

In general, I haven't found as many bluegills close to the dam, or even on the 'dam-side' break. Normally, more bluegills will be found on the break going from the shallow water into the deeper basin. You may not find the best fishing in the very deepest water, but pond bluegills are definitely oriented toward the deeper water during the iced-over period.

CHAPTER FIVE

PRESENTATION

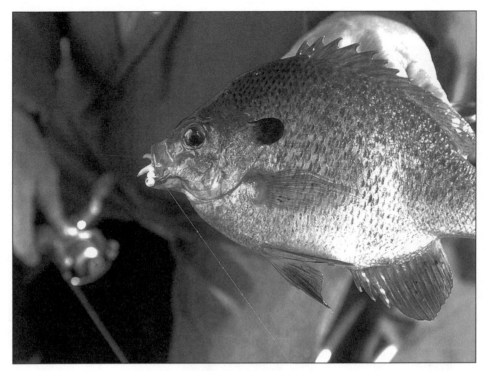

What did you catch 'em on?

How were you working it?

One of the universal truths of ice fishing is that you can't catch fish if you aren't over the top of them. Finding fish will always be the most important part of catching them. If you're in 10 feet of water doing the "right" presentation, and the bluegills are in 18 feet of water, guess how many you're going to catch?

Still, for many people, this is the fascinating part of fishing. Getting bluegills to bite, detecting the bite, setting the hook, and fighting the fish.

Just remember: this is important stuff, but it will never be as important as finding fish in the first place.

We're Talking Midday Here

We all become better ice fishermen at sunset. Then, the fish are actually eating, and they'll catch you and rip your rod out of your hand if you don't have a tight grip on it. Throughout this book, I'm not talking about prime-time fish. These are methods for catching bluegills during the midday period, when your presentation has to be too good, and too easy, for them to pass up.

During daylight hours, it's a battle of finesse against fish that really aren't in the mood to cooperate. You have to pay attention to detail to succeed.

Jig Styles

In my opinion, way too many anglers spend way too much effort trying to decide which of the many jig styles to choose from. In my experience, bluegills don't often bite one style jig while ignoring others. The factors affecting whether they bite or not are: how you work the jig, how fresh your bait is, and how well you threaded the live bait on the hook. Taken together, those factors can mean everything when it comes to triggering bites.

Again, if there is a secret to success, it's location, location, location, fresh maggies, fresh maggies, fresh maggies.

When it comes to jigs, I do have a strong preference for a horizontal presentation. You can easily tell which jigs offer a horizontal action—they're the ones with the eyelet coming up off the leadhead, rather than out the top of the head. I like a jig that swims naturally, in a horizontal attitude, especially in clear water.

(Tip: after you catch a fish, or even snag a weed, you need to re-position the knot so the jig hangs horizontally. When the knot gets pulled around the eyelet toward the top of the leadhead, a 'horizontal' jig will function more like a vertical jig.)

From the top: two Fat Boys, a Genz Worm, and a Pounder... small jigs that fish heavy.

As I mentioned in the System chapter (Chapter Two), I prefer 'small jigs that fish heavy,' that show up well on electronics. When I fish bluegills, I reach for a #12 or #10 System Tackle Fat Boy more than any other jig. They really help me perform a 'kicking' motion, and don't spin much. I choose the smaller size, most of the time, for shallow, clear water. The smallest Genz Worm is another horizontal jig that performs well.

Actually, I designed a series of panfish jigs for System Tackle, each made of a different shape and meant for a certain job. 'Copeds' are another good shallow-water jig. I often fish copeds with a 'jerk, fall back, jerk' motion. A real copepod, which they imitate, can swim quickly for a few feet and then they fall back.

'Fat Boys' and 'Pounders' fish heavy for their relative size, so they're also good for deeper water. Gram for gram, they show up better on your

---

depthfinder than other jigs, so I call them 'flasher friendly' jigs. In fact, because Pounders show up so well on my FL-8, I often use them in thick weeds even though they are not horizontal jigs. You can get an 'S-cable' as an accessory for the FL-8, and what it does is reduce the power of the unit, which reduces the clutter on your screen. By using an S-cable and a Pounder in thick weeds, you can see your jig on the screen, and know when it's down in pockets where the bluegills can see it. When the gap in the weeds turns red on the FL-8, you know a fish is looking at your jig.

Pounders can also be the ticket when deep fish want an aggressive 'pounding' presentation, because they tend to resist spinning more than any other jig I've fished. Fat Boys are a great horizontal swimming jig, and like I said, they're my all-around favorite for most bluegill fishing, in both shallow and deeper water situations.

The Advantage of 'Small & Heavy'

Jigs that are small in appearance but 'fish heavy' offer you a big advantage, because you can get up and down so much faster than somebody fishing with one of those almost-weightless numbers. You'll hear people argue that bluegills get so fussy they'll ignore a jig that comes down at them like a World War II bomb. That may be true, but it's important to realize that you can easily control how fast your jig falls by swimming it down on a tight line, no matter how much it weighs.

Like a puppeteer, you can make that jig look alive and almost weightless in the water. Let's say bluegills are biting at 16 feet over 18 feet of water. Let the jig drop quickly until it gets to 10 feet (by watching it sink on your depthfinder), then take control and fish it slowly down the rest of the way. As it enters the vision of the bluegills, you can make it do anything you want. Decide how they want it by experimentation, then repeat the jigging action they want.

Your overall goal is to fish efficiently, to get up and down as quickly as you can and still catch fish. If it takes a long time for your bait to sink into the fish zone, then a small bluegill hits and you don't hook it, you have to reel back up to make sure your bait is still on there. While you're slowly sinking that bait back down again, I'm in the fish zone with my relatively heavier jig.

The fact that the heavier jig sinks faster can work in your favor, because many times bigger bluegills can be the last ones in a group of fish to approach the jig. If your bait sinks super-slow, many times little fish get there first. If that's happening to you, it can help to sink a jig fast past the small fish and let it hit bottom, then fish your way up into the larger bluegills.

A big part of the story is shallow vs. deep fish, and clear water vs. dirty. Bluegills in clear water and shallow water are more sight oriented. At midday, those fish can be extremely difficult to catch. Your bait is more likely to have to have a certain motion. A lot of times, the bait can't be spinning around at all, and it often needs to have a kicking or swimming motion as it falls to the fish.

Deep-water bluegills, especially if the water is dirty, are generally daytime feeders. You don't catch them much in the evening. You catch 'em at high noon, and you can be more careless with your presentation. Drop it down to them and they'll still grab it, because they're feeding. Now you see the advantage of a small jig that fishes heavy. Get it up and down quicker and you'll catch more fish.

The bottom is not the bottom line

Yes, bluegills are often close to bottom. But not always, and fishing right on bottom, or inches off bottom, is not going to consistently catch the most fish. You'll see what depth most of the fish are, by closely watching your FL-8. Make sure you fish above the fish.

When anglers first start using an FL-8, they see a fish mark come on their display and it often seems to "rise" to meet the bait. It looks like you've coaxed the fish to come up off the bottom.

That's not what's happening, at least not most of the time. Most of the time, the fish is coming in from the side and getting closer and closer. The way sonar works, it looks like the fish signal is rising up to meet the bait, but in fact, the fish is coming from the side and just getting more directly beneath you.

When a fish first displays on your screen, it's on the outside fringe of your 'cone angle.' The signal hitting the fish—because the fish is off to the side—is traveling a longer distance than the signal that's simultaneously going straight down and bouncing off your lure. The fish is most likely at the same depth as your lure, even though it shows up "deeper" than the lure on your unit. As the fish continues to approach the lure, the sonar signals 'marking' the fish are traveling shorter and shorter distances, until the fish is right at the lure. At that point, the signals bouncing off the fish and the lure are traveling the same distance, and they virtually come together on your display.

This is a critical concept to understand.

Bluegills are usually more willing to come up to hit a bait than swim down (as are most fish). So don't be fooled into thinking you're fishing too shallow when you see fish 'rising up to meet your bait,' unless they're rising five or six feet or more. Try to fish slightly above the depth you think most of the fish are holding. Bluegills are accustomed to looking up to find food.

When I sight fish in clear water—meaning I'm in perhaps 10 feet or less—my most common depth to fish is 'halfway down.' I don't bury my jig in the weeds, or pound it off the bottom. I may work it up and down, occasionally bouncing it off bottom. But most of the time it will be about halfway between the bottom and the surface.

Again, the main lesson here is that fishing inches off the bottom is not going to consistently produce the most bluegills.

An Interview With Dave Genz on Presentation

This is your editor again, still holding to the belief that interviews are revealing, fascinating glimpses into the thought processes of great anglers. Here's the best stuff from our discussions on how to get bluegills to bite.

Q: *It's been said that bluegills appear, at least, to have more 'intelligence' or whatever you want to call it, than most freshwater fish species. Some people believe they learn to look up, and can see you in the hole, and they watch the jig come down, and unless it's perfect they aren't fooled into biting. Do you think bluegills are 'smarter' than other fish?*

Dave: In clear water, you definitely have to fish your way down, in a uniform method, like the thing is swimming or sinking slowly toward the bottom. When a bluegill sees it and moves toward it, you definitely don't want to flinch and change your presentation.

I learned this from sight fishing. When you see a fish coming, you have a tendency to stop and wait for the fish to bite it, and a lot of times that's all it takes for him to turn away from it, or miss it if he's timing your motion. It's hard to give fish smarts, but they do turn away from something if it doesn't keep moving the way they want it.

It does seem bluegills are interested in uniformity (in jigging actions). Even when I'm fishing deep-water fish, I tend to stop the freefall of my jig above the marks and start my presentation, so it comes kicking slowly down to them.

Q: *You use a wide variety of jigging motions, but do you have any routines you start with, a set program you run through at the beginning of a day, as you're trying to figure out how bluegills want the bait presented?*

Dave: Once you've zeroed in on the location of fish, you have the luxury of being able to fish more slowly, and maybe longer in one hole. At first, you have to effectively search. You've got to get that hole fished, and move on to another spot if you're not catching anything.

I think of it as casting through the ice. How many casts can I make by the end of the day? You have to drill holes in different depths, and you have to cover different depths in each hole.

I fish my way down, fish my way up, and keep doing that until I see a pattern.

Especially when you're working shallow water, slowly swim the bait downward as you let out line, a little at a time. Help your bait to swim, not spin. During the daylight hours, you're lucky if shallow-water bluegills are even in a neutral feeding attitude. They might eat if everything looks good, but if it's not right they'll just turn and swim away from it.

Whatever you do, don't get hung up on a set of moves; I've seen guys who always jiggle their baits the same way, whether they're catching fish or not.

On some days, a completely stationary presentation will be what it takes to trigger bites. Sometimes, you have to 'pound' (jig aggressively in very short movements, mainly from your wrist) the bait to get fish to come look at it, then stop it before they'll bite. Other times, you have to pound the bait and raise it slowly as you do. Other times, you have to pound and lower.

Other times, you have to jiggle in bigger movements, either slower or faster. Sometimes, it's critical that the bait is swimming in a horizontal attitude. We're convinced of the importance of a horizontal presentation in many situations, but there are still times when an aggressive vertical presentation will catch more fish.

Q: *How do you decide when to use which?*

Dave: It's a little more complicated than this, but a horizontal presentation is used to 'trick' fish. It really helps you catch fish that are lethargic and only respond to a bait after they get a chance to slide up and examine it. A vertical presentation is often used to 'trigger' fish that can be almost 'forced' to hit aggressive jigging. I don't think a jig that's hanging vertically looks as realistic to a fish as one that's hanging horizontally, so I fish aggressive with a vertical jig. This is what I've described as 'pounding,' using quick movements of the wrist (your hand looks like it's shaking, or 'nervous'). I keep it moving all the time, because I don't want the fish to get a good look at it.

I use a vertical jig, and 'pounding' under low-light conditions, in dirty water, in deeper water—any time fish can't see real well and have to get close to the bait before they can use visual clues. By keeping my bait moving, the fish have a hard time distinguishing whether it's real, and they have to hit it to find out.

Bluegills are curious. They want to check your bait out. They want to touch it, but they don't have arms, hands and fingers, so they have to use their mouth. By keeping the bait moving, you kind of force them to bite it if you get their curiosity up high enough.

When you're pounding it, you can jiggle-jiggle-jiggle, all the while raising or lowering it so it seems like it's escaping. You're trying to get the fish to chase the bait. I'm talking deep-water fish here. If you get them to move on it, usually they get to a certain point and they're committed, they believe the thing is getting away, and they'll take it. A lot of times, they all seem to bite at the same depth. Like they come in to look at it, you get 'em to chase it up 3 or 4 feet, and they hit.

Q: *Other than catching fish, what helps you decide which presentation to perhaps use more than others as you search?*

Dave: You watch your FL-8, especially when a fish comes on the screen. You know how you are working the bait, and you can watch how the fish reacts to it. Does the fish keep coming? Does it rush to the bait and hit? Does it sit there for a minute then fade away? Seeing this on your screen helps you decide whether to keep doing what you're doing or change to something else. That's why I call the FL-8 my mood indicator.

Q: *You've mentioned numerous times that bluegills usually don't like a jig to be spinning around. The fact is, especially when you're jiggling aggressively, the line develops twist and the bait spins around when you stop. What can you do to help prevent this?*

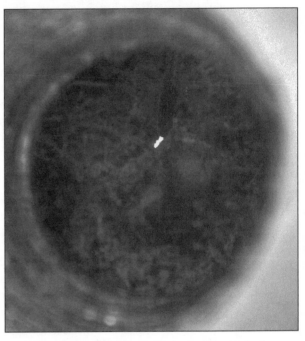

A nice bluegill sucks in the maggie end of a Genz Worm during a sight-fishing outing.

Dave: If you put three maggies on the hook at once, the bait won't spin around nearly as much. If your bait is spinning around as you jig, when you stop it unwinds forever, in front of any fish that are inspecting it. On many days, the fish won't hit it until it stops spinning, which can take a long time. By simply putting three maggies on each time you bait, you drastically cut down on this problem.

This spinning business is a problem with all types of bait, actually. Even wax worms, if they're not put on the hook straight, will cause the line to wind around in circles, and then it has to unwind.

If your line is getting twisted as you jig, hold the bait up when you bring it out of the water. Before you put the line back into the water, let it spin until it stops. This happens much more quickly when the line is above water than when it's under.

Q: *So putting three maggies on the hook, and threading a wax worm on straight, helps you avoid spin. But does that mean you always want to fish with three maggies? Do you ever prefer using one or two, or more than three?*

Dave: I would say I use three maggies—or one wax worm threaded on the hook—most of the time. But changing the number of maggies can change the action of the lure, and that can help catch fish on some days.

Sometimes, it's easier to change something on your lure than change your jigging motion. You get good at making your lure do some certain thing, and you can make subtle changes in the presentation by using more or fewer maggies. I suppose you could compare it to golf; you use pretty much the same swing, but change clubs to change how far you hit the ball, how high it goes, stuff like that.

In ice fishing, you kind of get your 'swing' down, the dabble as I like to call it, and by changing the style of lure or number of maggies on the hook, you can change how the lure behaves when you quiver, shake or pound it.

And one other thing: in some rare instances, we've bulked up our presentation by putting on as many as 10 maggies, like when we've been after bluegills up to two pounds and bigger.

Q: *You're known as a live-bait fisherman. What about the potential of artificials, including plastics, for bluegills through the ice?*

Dave: Plastics definitely have their place. Little Power Baits, and other tails, even flies suspended above or below an ice jig, will produce. Plastics are very popular in some places—in Wisconsin, for example. They catch fish. But do I believe bluegills ever eat plastics better than fresh live bait? Probably not.

Plastics are a great backup, an insurance policy, when you go out of town. You might forget your maggies or wax worms in the truck overnight and they all freeze. In that case, you might have to go to Plan B, and plastics can save the day. But I favor live bait, as long as it's lively and you keep putting fresh bait on through the day. Let's put it this way. I know what I fish with, and it's either maggies or wax worms most of the time.

Q: *You've said some good things about the potential, in some cases, for a more vertical presentation to catch bluegills. But I hear you talk about the importance of a horizontal presentation much more often. Can you get into more detail about why the horizontal attitude of the jig is important?*

Dave: During the midday hours, in shallow water, in clear water, the fish are going to get a good look at your presentation. And a horizontal presentation just looks more natural to a fish than a vertical one.

This is finesse fishing; we're not triggering strikes, we're trying to finesse strikes, to trick fish into believing our bait is real. If something looks natural, a fish will grab it. If it doesn't, they might swim up to it, but they'll swim away without eating it. If your bait is swimming naturally—horizontally—fish that can see well tend to approach it from farther away, and they don't seem to refuse it as often.

Q: *Tell us some more about the type of motion you're trying to impart to the jig, and how you achieve it.*

Dave: As I've played with horizontal jigging, I've discovered a few fine points:

• First, what you're trying to do is get a good 'kicking' motion when you jig, so the eye of the jig is the pivot point and the tail portion (the maggies or wax worm) kicks up and down like a horse's legs bucking. You don't want the entire jig to bounce up and down in high hops. The pivot point is just that; it doesn't move up and down much. It's like a rocking motion, from a horizontal position. We call it the 'Horizontal Rock.' This type of movement evidently looks natural, because we've had a lot of success with it. This is really important! You want that rocking, kicking motion to happen while the overall 'attitude' of the jig is horizontal.

• Second, I've modified my hand position to maximize the Horizontal Rock. My index finger curves over the top of the rod handle, as if I'm holding the reel like a pitcher holds a baseball. This will feel strange at first, but if you compare the action you get on the jig to how it behaves when you hold the reel in the traditional manner, you'll see how much more control you have.

Actually, with different types of reels, I've found I hold the reel a little differently, whatever it takes to feel comfortable and get that kicking motion.

Q: *And you've said that, at times, the bluegills want the bait dead still.*

Dave: Yeah, that's true, so sometimes, when I know fish are around the bait, I'll lay the rod down on my leg and see if they take it. The reel is laying on your leg, and the rod is light enough that the weight of the reel sort of sticks it to your leg.

A lot of times, that

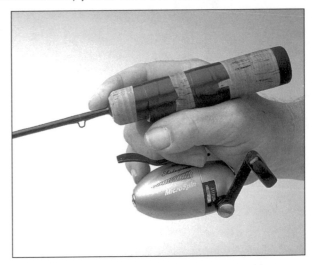

Here is one of the modified hand positions that Dave uses when jigging. Among other things, it enhances the 'Horizontal Rock' presentation. Different anglers have different size hands, which can mean it takes a slightly different hand position to feel comfortable.

will let the line unwind if it's twisted. Your lure will spin for a while, sometimes for a long time, it might go backwards a little bit, and then it stops. That can be the hardest presentation to do is stopped. To get the lure to totally stop moving. Sometimes, when it's spinning, the fish will sit inches away and wait for it to come to a complete stop before the suck it in.

Q: *How often is that the case? What percentage of the time do you think they want the bait completely still?*

Dave: I think they want it moving more often than they want it stopped.

Movement can be a key a lot of times, and we only have rising and falling as our main directions to go through a hole in the ice. You can swim it around the hole a bit, but up and down are the main options. Sometimes, the bugs leave the bottom and swim toward the top, and sometimes, they're at the top and moving toward the bottom. I just try both ways and see what works best.

I think you can get overly worked up about trying to know exactly what the fish are feeding on, and how that prey behaves in the water. All fish are opportunistic, and if your bait looks natural and smells natural, they'll eat it.

Q: *You've said in the past that ice anglers are overly concerned with what color jigs others are having success with. How important is color?*

Dave: The important things, in order of importance, are: depth, speed, and then color. If you see somebody catching fish, the first question out of your mouth should not be "what color do you have on?"

The most important thing is to fish at the right depth. What depth are the fish holding at?

Q: *How often is one specific depth a big key to catching bluegills?*

Dave: I think if they're in 18 feet of water, most of the fish in that area will be at 18 feet. There might be other fish in another part of the lake in another depth, but it can be a big factor. Sometimes the depth of water is structure to fish. What depth does the weedline occur at? Or what depth is plankton suspended at? A lot of times, I think it's a visibility thing; small fish might suspend at a depth where they're hard to see. Specific depths can be important.

This might not be part of this discussion, but it's worth noting that, whenever I'm catching bluegills, I seem to see suspended particles all over the screen on my FL-8. When I have a 'clean screen,' I don't usually catch fish. Sometimes you'll see little critters, zooplankton, swimming around in the hole. When you find life like that, you're going to find bluegills. Fish are where they are because they're near food. Catchable fish, that is.

'Speed,' just means what you're doing with your lure, how aggressive or slowly you're jigging. That's still more important than what color the lure is. I still say the biggest problem most people have is they use the same presentation all the time. And when they catch fish doing it, that just makes them more determined to keep using it all the time. You have to break out of that habit and experiment. That's why I depend so much on my FL-8. It's my eyes down there. It helps me determine, on a minute-by-minute basis, how the fish want the lure presented.

Color, often discussed at length, is rarely as important as depth and speed. Color is really a refinement you make after you have the other two factors under control. It makes no sense to change colors if you're not fishing where there's fish. And most of the time it's more important to get the presentation right than play with color.

But I will say this: for bluegills, I like air-brushed jigs better than the ones that are dipped into paint. With air-brushed jigs, you get a blending of colors, and shades that might be appealing to the fish. All things being equal, I usually have my best luck with orange and chartreuse, green and chartreuse, or glow for deep water, dirty water, and at night.

Q: *Do you jig differently when you see fish on your depthfinder compared to when you don't?*

Dave: If I don't see anything, I assume I'm trying to call fish in to my hole from a distance. Yeah, I probably use bigger jerks, ripping the bait up and down, making vibrations in the water, trying to get their attention. You want them to come your direction and see what this thing is.

If I'm not seeing fish, I fish more aggressively, or sometimes with bigger lures, flashier, brighter colors. Sometimes, when small fish and big fish are together in the same area, upsizing your lure can catch you bigger fish. Smaller is not always better. It's not that often, anymore, where we're sitting on a school of just big bluegills. All sizes are there, especially on pressured lakes. I've experienced it where, by putting on a bigger lure, or more bait—three wax worms or five maggies—I can keep the little ones away and give the big ones an opportunity to come in and grab it.

Sometimes, you have to figure out what's down there. I remember a situation on a lake in central Minnesota. Everybody was catching nothing but tiny bluegills, and we were seeing a solid band of these little fish on our screens. But if you got into a hole that didn't have that solid band of little fish, you caught bigger ones. I remember that pattern so well.

Q: *I keep getting stuck on this question: you say you fish aggressively when you're trying to find fish, and you don't have the luxury of slowing down until you locate fish. But what about the possibility that you won't attract bluegills into your hole, or trigger them, unless you fish slowly, unless your presentation is very subtle? Aren't you risking missing out on some fish with your approach?*

Dave: I don't really think so, because the FL-8 helps so much. It's a rare day when fish will be drawn in from a distance better with a subtle approach, and I'll see the fish when it enters the edge of my cone angle, and can work on it to see what it takes to bring the fish closer.

This might not apply if you are going back to a small area five days in a row. Some guys fish all winter in a spot as big as

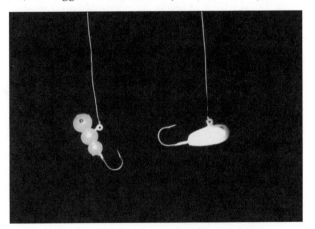

To achieve a horizontal presentation, a jig needs to have the eye coming out of the middle of the head. Both of these do. You often have to position the knot so it comes out of the middle of the eye (right), and re-position it every time you get snagged or catch a fish, or it looks like the jig at left, which would swim 'vertical.'

my garage; I realize that. If you know fish are around, you have the luxury of experimenting with your presentation even before you see fish. Overall, my approach is based on the assumption that I'm fishing a new area and don't know where the fish are ahead of time.

For me, it's a hunt. Sometimes, fishing is more like hunting than hunting is. When you're hunting, you can at least see the terrain with your own two eyes. When you're fishing, you're searching for fish in water, where you have to use a depthfinder, or an Aqua-Vu camera, as your underwater eyes. You have to be imaginative, and you have to play the odds, to catch the most fish. To beat the odds, fish aggressively until you encounter fish, then you can slow down if that's what it takes to catch more than just a few eager biters.

Q: *Help us all understand what a subtle bite from a bluegill feels like. Sometimes, when we're sight fishing, even a big fish takes the jig all the way in and it seems like you don't feel a thing. How do we know we're not missing tons of bites when we can't see our hook?*

Dave: A good rod, like we talked about in the System chapter, is a big deal. And so is thin, fresh line that hangs straight. You have to be able to feel the jig, feel the weight of the jig, even though it doesn't weigh much.

A lot of times, when I can't see the bait, I jig the rod so the lure is going 'thunk-thunk-thunk' and I can feel it. I'm not going to kid people and say it's easy to learn this, but you can develop your sense of feel with practice. It's more subtle than if you were jigging with a 1/4-ounce jig, so you have to tune into it.

The absence of the weight of the jig is the bite sometimes. You feel it, feel it, feel it, and then it's gone all of a sudden and you set the hook. As for your sight fishing, a lot of people see the fish come in, and they know they're about to bite. They instinctively drop their rod tip to the fish, sort of giving the bait to him. That's partly why you don't feel anything, because there's slack in the line. I've tested this, by closing my eyes when I see a fish come into my hole, and feeling for the bite. If you keep the line tight, you feel the bites a lot easier.

It's those fish that cruise into your hole, suck in the bait, and keep going that are hard to detect. All you feel is the line tightening up as they swim away, assuming they haven't spit it out yet. When they stop and suck it in, that's when you feel that sharp 'tick.'

I'm sold on good graphite rods, but some people like other bite-detection aids, like a spring bobber. A spring bobber is a good bite detector, but it can limit your style of jigging because it 'softens' the tip of your rod. A good float is a great bite detector, too, but it sometimes restricts your up-and-down movement. For presentation, I like just my bait hanging down below a rod, without the spring tip or float. But the best bite detector can be what you're used to, what you like, what works for you.

Fishing in a Fish Trap, or any shelter, helps bite detection, because it takes away the wind, which can blow your line around. Plus, it helps your concentration. You seem to be able to zone in on your bait and what's happening, and it's amazing how sensitive you become. You can line your rod tip up with something, like the edge of your FL-8 face, and watch the display and see if your rod tip moves the slightest bit. Or, balance the rod on your leg, so it pivots if you get a bite.

Whatever you do, don't use a wimpy rod. It kills me when people call those flexible rods 'sensitive.' They're the opposite of sensitive. Get a rod you can feel bites with, or use a spring bobber or float, whatever works best for you.

Q: *Okay, let's assume we got a bite and it's time to set the hook. Teach us the right way to put the hook home.*

Dave: When you set the hook, it's a mistake if the rod ends up above your head.

If that happens, now you're trying to wind fast enough to get the rod back down in front of you, and in the meantime, the fish is in control. You have to keep the whole works out in front of you.

No matter how cool it looks on TV, don't use your shoulders and arms to set the hook. It's a wrist thing. It's a snap of the wrist thing.

With the right rod, a rod that has a flexible tip but good backbone, you can set the hook with a very short movement. A long movement, that uses your arms and shoulders, is extremely slow, and gives the fish time to spit out the hook. You might think you're being very decisive, very aggressive, if you really pump the rod upward until it hits the roof of your Fish Trap, but you aren't. You're actually giving the fish more time to react.

A quick flip of the wrist will bring into play the power of the rod, and will drive the hook home. Even with a 'lightweight' panfish rod, if the blank has the right power curve, you can literally turn a fish over on its side with just an upward turn of your wrist.

Q: *Okay, let's assume we got the hook driven home. Now the fight begins. Teach us how to get the fish into the hole without losing it.*

Fishing inside a portable shelter, like this Fish Trap, helps your concentration level, because it blocks out distractions. That helps you detect subtle bites of bluegills. The walls block the wind, which helps you watch your line for any sign of movement.

Dave: The most common mistake after the fight begins is letting the rod come to 'rest,' which creates slack in the line. As long as the rod is bent it's 'loaded,' and the fish is under your control. If the flex comes out of the rod, the fish can get slack line, and if you didn't get a good hookset, it's easy for the fish to get off.

Remember, the rod should have a flexible tip, which will help cushion the shock if the fish makes a sudden run. Your reel should either have a good drag system, or a way for you to backreel and give line.

Don't get into the habit of pumping the rod upward and then dropping it down to reel up the slack line. You can pump upward as long as you keep continuous tension on the rod. If you drop the rod quickly and create slack, you're begging for the fish to get off.

Also, be patient. Enjoy the fight. Too many people are in a hurry to land the fish and get back to fishing. If you take your time and fight the fish, you'll have more fun and land more. Horsing a fish can cause any number of bad things to happen, including having the hook come out from too much pressure, or having the line break from a sudden shock exceeding the breaking strength.

By the way, dull hooks are another major cause of losing fish. Carry a fine file and touch up even your tiny little panfish jigs, and you'll get deeper hooksets, and land more fish.

And be patient when the fish gets to the hole. Keep the rod bent, and keep everything under control, and eventually the fish will be coming up close to the hole. Now we have to get the fish's head started up the hole. It's again at this point when a lot of anglers get impatient, and start to break every rule of fighting fish.

I see guys reach down into the hole and grab the fish too soon, or even drop their rods and try to grab the fish. I also see people grab the line and try to lift the fish by the line, which causes many breakoffs and also makes it easy for the fish to shake the hook loose.

A fish may not be 'smart,' but it knows it doesn't want to go up the hole. If the fish's nose gets past the outside edge of the hole, let it swim by and turn it for another try. If you try to force the fish up the hole from a bad angle, that's often the cause of the hook catching on the bottom of the ice.

Also, be ready for a surge of strength once they get into the hole. They struggle hard, even if they seem whipped. Remain calm, and try to get their head started up the hole. Keep this in mind: once they start coming up the hole, they can't turn around and swim down, unless they are quite a bit smaller than the hole.

Once the fish's head is at the top of the ice, you can reach down and grab it, or just slide the fish onto the ice if it's small enough. But at no time should you allow the flex to come out of the rod until the fight is won. A couple years ago, Mark Strand caught a 2-pound, 8-ounce bluegill in Nebraska, and his story of the fight is enough to make you a believer.

Once the fish started up the 7-inch hole, it stuck good. The head was all the way out of the water, but this beautiful trophy was far from landed. It was a Mexican standoff for a while, but Mark held his ground, kept the rod bent and the line tight, and soon enough the fish tried to 'jump,' and it propelled itself neatly out of the hole and flopped on the ice in his Fish Trap. Had Mark tried to grab the line it no doubt would have broken. Had he let up on the rod, the fish could have slid back down the hole. The power of a good rod brought the battle to a successful conclusion.

How to Get Good Bait for Ice Fishing

Fresh live bait on your hook is a key to catching fish, more important than most anglers will ever know. If you hook the bait properly, "juices" are released into the water that I believe strongly influence a bluegill's desire, and willingness, to bite.

Change your bait frequently during the day. I've probably left the same bait on my hook for up to 15 minutes—if the bait looks good and I'm mainly using the sight of it to draw fish into the hole, and it's a nice day when the bait isn't likely to freeze. But when a fish comes in the hole, now we're into flavor and scent as primary triggers, and I want fresh bait on there. On average, changing bait every 5 minutes or so is probably more like it for me.

Actually, it's hard to put a time limit on how long you leave the same bait on. Some days, you fish one hole for a few minutes and move to the next hole, and the bait freezes while it's out of the water. So you might change every 3 minutes then.

There is good live bait and so-so live bait. At some bait shops, they aren't as committed to keeping only the freshest bait in stock.

That's why you need to travel around to all the bait stores in your area and get a good sense for where the best bait is available. Multi-colored maggies are probably my number-one bluegill choice, but they have to be kept cold enough that they don't begin to harden into casings before their time. And wax worms should be fresh and lively, too, not sunken-looking like they get after spending too much time in the bait store waiting to be purchased.

If you ask around enough, you can find out who the growers are in your area, and you might consider teaming up with your friends to buy mass quantities and split them up. That way, you know when they were purchased.

If you can't find the right bait in your area, there is one good dealer that I have had lots of personal contact with, that I can recommend to you. Express Bait in Minnesota (800-451-2576) can ship you Maggies (multi-colored larvae, sometimes called spikes, silver wigglers, or maggots), wax worms, wigglers (mayfly larvae), freshwater shrimp, meal worms, mousies, and other baits that are popular in certain regions, and they'll arrive in good shape.

How to Hook Maggies and Wax Worms

You must keep fresh live bait in front of bluegills to consistently catch them! And how you hook maggies and wax worms on your jig is critical to catching fish.

Maggies have a sharp, pointed end and a 'fat' end. Find the fat end and make sure it's pointing out where you can pierce it with the hook. Now, roll the maggie between your thumb and index finger and press lightly so the maggie 'bulges,' and hook it as lightly as you can through the end of the bulge. Clear juices should flow. If juices the color of the maggie come out, you've hooked it too deeply.

Hooked this way, you can often see the hook through the skin of the maggie, and the bait will wiggle well (how well depends on how cold they are). Put on more maggies if you want, then quickly get the bait in the water and start fishing it. After about five minutes, if you haven't had a bite, change the bait.

Thread wax worms on the hook. First, pull off the black head on one end by piercing it with the hook and tearing it free. That will allow you to easily thread the hook on through the new opening. Make sure it goes on straight, or your jig will wobble and spin when you jiggle it.

Hook maggies very lightly through the fat end (left). A thin, sharp hook is a must, and it helps to pinch down the barb for easier penetration. Hook a wax worm (right) by first using the hook to 'tear off' the black head from one end, then thread the waxie on the hook, being careful to keep it sliding on straight. You'll notice that the knot has slid around on the maggie-laden jig; in order to keep that jig fishing horizontally, you would first have to bring the knot around so it hangs off the center of the eyelet. The wax worm jig on the right is ready to fish horizontally.

CHAPTER SIX

MISC. THOUGHTS

Stuff to think about...

When you try to lay out 'rules' for fishing bluegills through the ice, you think of lots of exceptions every time you say anything. But that shouldn't keep us from trying to understand why we catch fish one day and struggle the next.

The more comfortable you become with the basics, the more you notice the details, like how weather impacts your fishing success. Let's look at a few variables that can affect your pursuit of 'gills.

Light Levels

Is the day sunny or cloudy? Is it midday, or early or late in the day? Are you fishing through a thin sheet of clear ice, or a thick blanket of snow over a thick plate of cloudy ice?

The amount of light penetrating the ice has a huge impact on bluegill fishing. I would rather fish deep-water 'gills, for instance, on a sunny day, when they can see better. There's enough light down there for them to feed efficiently, and it seems to get them in the mood to forage.

If I'm sight fishing in shallow, clear water, I like a day that's cloudy, or the low-light portions of the day. That seems to embolden bluegills to roam more, and feed more actively.

Macro Weather

Pay attention to the big picture when it comes to weather.

Look at the entire summer and fall. Did the weeds grow well, or not so well, in your area lakes? This is related to whether we've had a 'sunny year' or 'cloudy year,' warm year or cool year, generally speaking. What condition are the weeds in going into ice-up? It makes a difference, in terms of whether bluegills will use the weeds or not during the ice-fishing season.

Once the winter begins, notice overall trends as compared with other years. Have we had lots of snow this year, or not so much? Remember, lots of snow means less light penetration (which can be a good thing, early in the season, but can reduce oxygen in the shallows as winter wears on, forcing bluegills into deeper water).

The weather, from a long-term perspective, makes a huge difference in what bluegills do—in what all fish do, and in what shape the overall underwater environment is in. Different food sources become relatively more or less abundant depending on long-term weather trends. Cooler, cloudier weather might make ideal hatching conditions for some bluegill prey items and not others. Sunny, warmer summers might create a boom in certain categories of bluegill food.

Do I have this all figured out? Heck no. Nobody knows everything about why fish do what they do. But I pay attention to it, and it helps me come up with theories as to where I should fish, and keeps me searching, deeper, shallower, in the weeds, on the flats, on the basin, until I find the fish I'm looking for.

Micro Weather

There isn't a subject related to fishing that brings on more opinions than the impact of short-term weather changes on the mood of fish. But it seems like the discussion gets tabled once the lakes freeze over and it's time to go ice fishing.

Changing weather patterns affect ice fishing, too. I don't have any scientific studies to cite, but experiences fishing many days in a row with a lot of really good anglers, have led me to some opinions and theories.

(A lot of what I have to say here comes from observations made while chasing 'gills in the midwinter period in places where the winter is long, and snow covers the ice.)

The first thing that comes to mind is a difference between bluegills and perch, although crappies can fall in here, too. It seems like if the bluegills aren't biting, the perch are. For instance, I've noticed a lot of times that bright, high-pressure days might turn off the bluegills, but turn on the perch. And, vice versa, sometimes on a cloudy day the perch don't seem to be biting, but you can switch over to chasing bluegills and catch 'em.

It's something to look for.

Cold Fronts

In my mind, what cold fronts really mean is more sunlight coming through into the water (although if you live in regions where significant amounts of snow remain on the ice for weeks or months, that cuts light penetration severely, and the effect may not be as drastic). In my experience, after the front moves through, many fish seem to tuck up into weeds or other cover (such as brush) if it's available.

As the front's moving in, I've seen fish show a tendency to move away from weeds (or other forms of cover), onto open-water flats. When you fish 10 days in a row on the same body of water, in the same general area, you get to see what happens as the weather changes.

Weather Changes Mean Fish Movement

One thing that's clear—no matter what species you're talking about—is that, as the weather changes, fish just generally move. Don't expect to catch fish out of the same hole day after day, even if you're quiet and careful and don't think fishing pressure, by itself, is sufficient to make them move.

Weather conditions can make fish move—in and out of cover, up and down the dropoff. Lots of things can happen! You have to go out with the attitude that if something changes, you might have to go looking for the fish all over again.

This is a big mistake many anglers make. If you catch fish one day, then the weather changes and you go back to those same holes and don't even see fish on your depthfinder, don't say the fish aren't biting. React. Go looking for them. They didn't swim all the way across the lake. They're not far. A lot of times, you can find them again if you search. And once you locate them, you might have to change your presentation to get them to bite.

Realize that the whole underwater world changes as things go from cloudy to sunny, from high pressure to low pressure. The whole world 'under there' reacts to the changes.

You may have to start up your search again, even if you think you've nailed down a hot spot and caught fish from it four days in a row. When you go back into search mode, you have to rely on your electronics to find them, then judge their mood.

Get over the fish, then see whether they'll bite on what you're offering. If they don't, change things up. And I don't mean just change the color of the jig. Change things up in a bigger way than that. Get more aggressive, or less aggressive. Change the type of live bait. See what they want.

Don't just give up.

Try to stay confident. Believe the fish will bite, assuming you can find them and give them what they want. If you have to leave and haven't caught anything, tell yourself you ran out of time—not that the fish weren't biting.

Feeding Sprees

Pay attention for what we might call a 'feeding spree' to break out at any time of day, for no apparent reason. We've all experienced this. You've had a fish on your FL-8 display for a while and all of a sudden it bites. You catch three or four fish in a row, and then they quit. You get back together with your buddies a couple hours later and you find out everybody caught fish during that same time period.

I don't believe the fish 'moved.' I don't think a 'wave' of fish comes through. They just get active for some reason, and it must be connected to something in the environment, whether it's an activity period for zooplankton, related to forces like barometric pressure or moon cycles, or who knows what.

Moon Cycles and Feeding Periods

Laugh all you want. During the week of the new moon phase (the dark of the moon), when there's no moon at night, that definitely makes bluegills better midday feeders. When I'm going on a run to check out new lakes, I try to time it for this period, to give me the best chance of catching whatever lives there.

We pay attention to moon rise and moon set, too. There seems to be something there. The moon cycles, and the moon's influence on fishing, is an area that we should all pay more attention to.

Noise

You're expecting me to say that noise is the enemy at all times, but the story may not be as simple as that.

Time of year is a big thing when it comes to noise. If you were going to generalize, noise and moving shadows spook bluegills at early ice, but late in the year noise can actually get 'gills moving and help you catch them.

Where you're fishing makes a big difference, too. In clear, shallow water, where the fish can see shadows or perhaps even see you up there, movements and noise can be a problem. There have been times when leaving the slush in the hole and just 'drilling' a pencil-size hole with the rod tip, for the jig to go through, results in more fish.

You might be surprised to hear me say that I think anytime after midwinter, a bit of noise can work to your advantage.

I'm talking midday again now. If the fish are there and you're catching them, you don't want those fish to move, so that's not the time to make noise. But if you're not catching or seeing anything, making noise sometimes can't hurt. This is another Aqua-Vu camera observation now, but I've seen numerous times when using the auger to drill some new holes actually seemed to trigger fish movements.

Somebody near you drills a hole, suddenly you see herds of fish coming through your hole, and they bite. After a while it gets quiet again, and you see nothing and catch nothing. Start the auger up again, drill a few holes, and you move the fish around and catch a few more.

Again, it's important that you realize I'm talking midday. These fish are not actively roaming, looking for food. They may be willing to bite if they get moved and see your bait, though. At prime time, when the bluegills are moving on their own, keeping noise to a minimum may be more important.

There seems to be a limit to how deep the fish can be and still get moved around by noise. In deep water, you have to keep looking until you find fish. In shallow water, you can move them around. Especially at the latter stages of the winter, getting the fish moving can be enough to create action.

Underwater Currents

I drive myself nuts wondering why bluegills are clustered in a certain area, and nearby areas—which seem at least similar, if not identical—don't have any fish.

Underwater currents may be at least part of the answer.

We've all experienced times when our line gets moved to one side of the hole, no matter how hard we try to keep it in the center. Obviously, there's a current moving in that direction. I've even seen it where my jig gets moved out of the cone angle of my depthfinder, and becomes hard to keep track of.

If a current is moving in a certain direction, algae and zooplankton get moved in that direction, too (although some species can move against currents, or position to minimize drifting), which can gather bluegills as they move with the food source. Then, everything comes to a spot where it stops. Current breaks happen in the winter under the ice. You keep moving around the lake, and eventually you come to a spot where your line is no longer pushed along by the current.

Temperature gradients are known to cause this. If, for example, the water near the surface warms to 4 degrees C, it sinks. On big waters, planetary rotation can be a factor. Whatever the cause on a local level, underwater currents seem to influence bluegill location. This is a factor that I've just begun to study, so there should be more to say in the future.

For now, maybe just tuck it into your mind as something to look for.

CHAPTER SEVEN

A FUTURE FOR BIG BLUEGILLS

We all want to catch big bull bluegills. But most of us catch small ones, most of the time.

That's reality. What will it take to ensure that at least some big bluegills are around for future generations? Or, even better, what would it take to increase the number of big bluegills in the future?

It's a question that biologists, as well as anglers, ask. There are theories, and there have been studies trying to determine what it would take to allow more bluegills to get bigger.

• Thin the weeds, so predators like northern pike can more efficiently thin the numbers of small bluegills. Didn't seem to work.

• Increase the relative abundance of predators like northern pike, so natural processes will trim the overall number of bluegills. Didn't seem to work either.

• In one recent study, it's been proposed that it's the age at which male bluegills become sexually active (which apparently severely slows their future growth rate, even if they grew quickly up to that age) that goes a long way toward determining the average size bluegill in a population. If there are larger males to drive smaller males away from nesting sites—especially the critical central core of nesting colonies—the smaller males won't become sexually active until they get older and bigger. If male bluegills are larger at the point their growth rate slows, that makes for larger overall fish in the population.

If this latest theory proves to have merit, it only strengthens my personal beliefs on what it will take to improve the average size of the bluegills we all catch.

I remember the 1960s, when bluegill fishing became more popular than ever. We were fishing these lakes in northwestern Minnesota, and there were hundreds of people fishing these 'gills, and there were huge numbers of honest pounders. Pretty soon, there were only 3/4-pounders, and then half-pounders, and soon after that, the lakes were full of these little stunted bluegills.

If we would have never removed those big bluegills from the population, would they have stunted anyway? I don't think so.

I think about Sunrise Lake, near the Twin Cities of Minneapolis and St. Paul. It was full of good, medium-sized bluegills. They opened it up to the public because it was such good fishing, and charged a fee. People gladly paid it, and left with their buckets of fish. They were within the legal limits, but they came in and harvested that crop, and now the lake is full of these 4-ouncers. People say the big bluegills 'will come back,' Well, wrong. There's already been plenty of time for them to get back to half-pound status if that was going to happen by itself.

I think about farm ponds, stock dams, whatever you want to call them. On one property, nobody can fish, because it's private and the owner doesn't let anyone in. A mile away is a very similar pond, open to the public. The public pond has little bluegills in it, and the private one has big ones.

It's no real mystery.

I'm not saying that I haven't been guilty, in the past, of keeping too many big bluegills. But I don't do it anymore, and I would only hope that the majority of other ice anglers could learn to do the same thing. Our limits are too generous. Think about keeping enough fish for one fresh meal, no freezing, no giving them away to the neighbors. No stopping to show the pile in order to make yourself feel like you tamed the wilderness.

Just because you're legally allowed to keep a high number of bluegills, and there is no size restriction, does that mean you have to reach that magic power word 'limit?' Can you have a satisfying experience letting the biggest ones go, and keeping the smaller ones to eat?

I can.

When a lake gets to the point where it's balanced, with a good number of large adult bluegills in it, the adult fish keep the number of juvenile fish under control. But when we harvest the big bluegills—when they go home in buckets—that allows the number of small fish to increase to the point that the system has very few big fish in it. It becomes a losing cycle, because anytime somebody does happen to catch a decent bluegill out of a stunted population, it immediately goes in the bucket as a symbol of triumph.

We find every other thing to blame bad fishing on. Blame the carp. Blame the pelicans and cormorants, because they're such efficient predators. It's time for us to face the fact that fishing pressure, and unwise keeping of large adult bluegills, is responsible for the creation of stunted populations.

Think about that next time you land a big one.

A Future for Big Bluegills

CHAPTER EIGHT

ICE SAFETY

"I think we can take this as a sign that it's still too early for ice fishing."

Move more and catch more fish.

Be mobile. But be careful.

Throughout this book, we stress the importance of being mobile on the ice.

Move more and you catch more fish.

That doesn't mean we want you to ignore ice safety while you're out there.

Ice conditions are going to vary from spot to spot on the same lake, and tremendously from region to region in the ice belt. In certain locales, ice thick enough to support foot traffic will only remain for several days or weeks at a time. That's why, above all else, you have to keep your safety in mind at all times.

If you feel at all uncertain about the ice conditions, wear a life jacket while you're ice fishing. It never gets discussed in the media, but what better way to ensure your safety? We've never heard of anyone falling through the ice and drowning while wearing a life jacket. (Although one side note here: about the only time experts say the use of a life jacket might not be a good idea, in an ice fishing situation, is when you're riding inside a vehicle on the ice; the life jacket might hamper your efforts to get out of the vehicle should it break through the ice. But once you get to the spot and start fishing, or while you're walking out to a spot, a life jacket can provide additional peace of mind—and support in an emergency.)

In general, we think 'flotation' clothing is going to become a staple with ice anglers, because the fabrics they're made with are now supple enough to wear comfortably in cold weather.

Bluegills!

Here are some recognized guidelines for knowing when ice is safe enough to support various modes of mobility, from the Minnesota Department of Natural Resources (DNR):

• Wait to walk out until there is at least 4 inches of clear, solid ice. True, thinner ice will support one angler, but ice thickness can vary just a few yards away, from the influence of flocks of waterfowl, water chemistry and local climate.

• Snowmobiles and ATVs need at least 5-6 inches of good ice.

• Automobiles and light trucks need 8 inches to a foot of good ice. But there's more to safely driving a vehicle on ice!

Keep a distance between vehicles, and don't follow each other single file (except when you have to, such as when roads are plowed out to fishing areas). When ice is only marginally safe for vehicle traffic, your car or truck makes a wake under the ice. When the wakes of more than one vehicle collide, cars following in close proximity can easily break through ice that safely held the leading cars! Also, no matter how thick the ice is, it's a good idea to drive slowly. A fast-moving vehicle can make a big bulge ahead of itself, and the ice can—it rarely happens, but it can—break apart in front of the fast-moving vehicle.

Obviously, avoid driving into known bad-ice areas, such as springs, moving water, and around aerators. Ask about each lake before you drive on. Also, and this can pertain to walking as well, avoid expansion cracks, or 'pressure ridges' as they are sometimes called. They are often easy to see. The ice expands and pushes over the top of itself, creating layers of broken ice. They can be like trap doors, especially where three of them converge.

Be prepared to bail out of a vehicle should it go through. Unbuckle your seat belt, and leave the windows rolled down if you suspect unsafe ice.

• Any time you're driving a vehicle or snowmobile, watch out for the large blocks of ice sometimes left laying around after large spearing or angling holes are sawed out. After snow covers them up, they can be impossible to see—another reason to drive slowly on ice.

(If you cut such a hole, by the way, either force it down under the ice and off to the side, or break it into little pieces.)

• Get or make a set of "picks" for helping yourself onto safe ice should you fall through. In European countries, use of picks is mandatory in ice-fishing contests. Several types are on the market and available at bait shops or through mail-order catalogs like Cabela's and Bass Pro Shops.

To make your own, take two short sections (about 4 1/2 to 5 inches) of old broom handle or 1-inch dowel. Remove the head of two good-sized nails. Drill a hole in the end of each dowel long enough to seat the unsharpened end of the nail. Glue the nails in each dowel and tie them together with about 2 1/2 feet of cord. It's a good idea to jab the sharp ends of the nails into small corks, which will break apart easily when you start jabbing the nails into the ice.

Wear the spikes around your neck any time you're unsure of ice conditions. In a minute, we'll get into using them to pull yourself to safety in an emergency.

All ice is not created equal

Several factors affect how solidly ice freezes on any given year, according to Sgt. Dave Branley of the Dane County (WI) Sherrif's Department. Sgt. Branley, with more than 30 years on the force, has been in charge of patrolling his county's waters, summer and winter, since 1980.

"We need about 6 inches of solid ice before we get the first heavy snowfall on it," Branley says. "If ice is just starting to be made and then snow falls on it, the weight of the snow pushes the ice down and can insulate it against ever freezing well."

Your best insurance against getting too far out on unsafe ice, experts agree, is to monitor local media for updates on the current year's ice conditions, and to talk with local resorts and bait shops, who will know about potential thin ice areas (you need a few ice flies and some Maggies or wax worms anyway, right?).

Ice thickness, in and of itself, is not a guarantee of smooth sailing late in the year. "Travel on ice is always at your own risk," says Branley, "and you should never assume ice is completely safe. But this is especially true toward spring. I know, the fishing gets great at last ice, but be careful out there. You look out and one day there's a lot of water on the ice, and the next day it's completely dry. The ice gets honeycombed and rotten, and eventually you can poke a 2x4 through 8 inches of ice, which used to be enough to support a vehicle."

What if you do go through?

Sometimes, no matter how careful you are, things happen. If you should fall through the ice while walking:

• Don't panic. Easier said than done, but it's fairly easy in most cases to get back up on the ice than you think. Go back the way you came from (you know the ice was thick enough to support you back there).

• All that heavy clothing will actually help you stay afloat if you don't start flailing away. Kick and fight to keep going forward; your feet will want to float up and you'll tend to fall backwards. If you have picks along, now's the time to use them. Get one in each hand and dig them alternately into the ice and pull yourself forward. To get onto good ice, roll away from the hole, or continue to work with the picks, sliding ahead on your belly (don't get up and start walking or you might break through again).

• Get to a heat source immediately and get those wet clothes off! If at all possible, get to a medical facility to be checked for signs of hypothermia and/or other trauma.

• If you see someone go through, designate one person to go for help, and another person to attempt the rescue. Don't walk right up to the victim and offer them your hand; that usually results in two people in the water. Build a chain with anything you can find: a snowmobile suit, hand auger, your belt, etc. Lay down and extend the 'chain' to the victim. Get secure and help pull them out of the hole, encouraging them to kick hard and stay down.

Your chances of breaking through the ice are slim indeed. If you follow these precautions and your own common sense, you'll always leave the lake as dry as you arrived.